BERMUDA

Other titles in the *Islands* series

Cyprus
Gibraltar
Island of Bute
Isle of Wight
Jersey
Kintyre
Majorca
Minorca
Harris & Lewis new edition
Isle of Arran
Rhodes
Uists and Barra
The Falkland Islands new edition
Lundy new edition
Orkney new edition
Shetland new edition
Aran Islands

Islands

BERMUDA

John J. Jackson

David & Charles
Newton Abbot London

Hippocrene Books Inc.
New York

For
Barbara and Thurston Hunt

All illustrations were provided by the Bermuda Department of Information Services.

British Library Cataloguing in Publication Data

Jackson, John J.
Bermuda.—(Islands series)
1. Bermuda Islands—History
I. Title II. Series
972.99 F1636

ISBN 0-7153-8921-1

Typeset by Typesetters (Birmingham) Ltd
Smethwick West Midlands
Printed in Great Britain
by Redwood Burn Limited Trowbridge Wilts
for David & Charles Publishers plc
Brunel House Newton Abbot Devon

Published in the United States of America
by Hippocrene Books Inc
171 Madison Avenue, New York, NY 10016

ISBN 0-87052-497-6 (United States)

CONTENTS

1 PHYSICAL ENVIRONMENT

In the opening of his lovely poem, Andrew Marvell extolled the wonders of Bermuda with:

Where the remote Bermudas ride
In the ocean's bosem unespied,
From a small boat that rows along
The listening winds received this song:

What should we do but sing his praise
That led us through the watery maze
Unto an isle so long unknown,
And yet far kinder than our own? . . .

Similarly when writing in 1613 the *Plaine Description of the Barmvdas*, Silvester Jourdan was inspired by the islands to quote Ecclesiastes 3:11 with 'God hath made every thing beautiful in his time.' On the other hand, Shakespeare called the group of islands 'The still vexed Bermoothes.' Why he so thought may be explained in the physical descriptions below or in Chapter 2. For now, it is probably best to settle into reading this book with Mark Twain's advice in mind. He found his creative spirit renewed on numerous trips to Bermuda and said, 'You go to Heaven if you want – I'll just stay here.'

LOCATION

Since Bermuda appears as nothing more than a dot on a world map, a traveller in a modern air or sea vessel may wonder how the islands will ever be found in that 'watery maze' in the western North Atlantic Ocean. Fortunately, navigators know that the Bermuda islands are located between latitude 32′15″N to 32′23″N and longitude 64′38″W to 64′15″W. This places Bermuda approximately 917 km (570 miles) east of Cape Hatteras, North Carolina. Alternatively, New York City is close to 1,245 km (774 miles) to the northwest and London is about 5,627 km (3,497 miles) to the northeast. Often erroneously classified as being in the West Indies, Bermuda is actually nearly 1,287 km (800 miles) north of the nearest West Indian island.

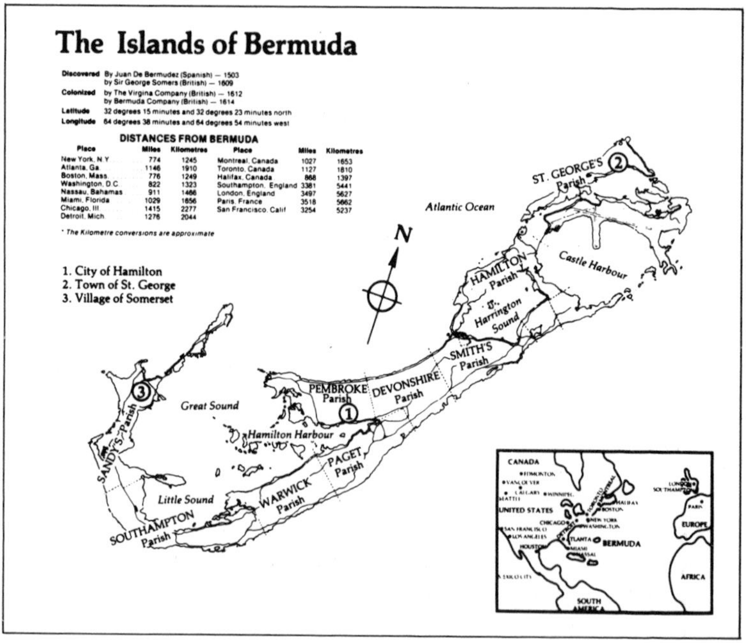

The Islands of Bermuda

The Bermuda Islands, usually referred to in the singular Bermuda, consist of about 150 islands and islets extending northwest to southwest in a fish-hook shaped chain along the edge of an extinct, submarine volcano. Twenty of the islands are inhabited and the seven principal ones – St. George's, St.

David's, the Main, Somerset, Watford, Boaz, and Ireland – are connected by bridges or causeways to form a chain about 35.4 km (22 miles) long and from 0.8 km (½ mile) to approximately 3.22 km (2 miles). The average width is less than 1.61 km (1 mile) and the total land area is 53.35 sq km (20.59 sq miles). By comparison, the land of Greater New York City is 15 times larger, and that of Greater London is 32 times more than Bermuda.

Reputable reference sources state that there are up to 365 islands in the Bermudas! Presumably this is because there are islets, rocks, banks, and shoals which may or may not always be counted or seen. Thus, most likely, the many who have been shipwrecked would agree with Shakespeare and find the islands vexed.

GEOLOGY AND RELIEF

Bermuda forms one of the northernmost groups of coral islands in the world and consists principally of windblown calcareous deposits capping a submerged and bevelled volcanic cone which rises more than 4,270 m (14,000 ft) from the floor of the Atlantic.*

Research is ongoing to try to pinpoint the ages of the various geological strata but it is believed that the first volcanic eruption occurred 100 million years ago and that, approximately 35 million years ago, a second eruptive period caused a huge volcano to form, the remnants of which are now Bermuda. In fact, three isolated volcanic peaks with fairly flat platforms at their apexes were formed. The southern submerged two are the Challenger Bank and the Argus Bank (or Plantagenet); each is about 90.67 sq km (35 sq miles) in area and at a depth of 61 m (200 ft). To the north, and ten times larger, is the Bermuda Bank along the eastern side of which are the islands of Bermuda.

If the sea level fell 15.24 m (50 ft) most of the platform would be revealed and so indicate the biological origins of Bermuda. This is because the volcanic origin is not visible but instead, covering the whole platform, is a fantastic assortment of coralline and calcareous algae. The algae proliferate on the

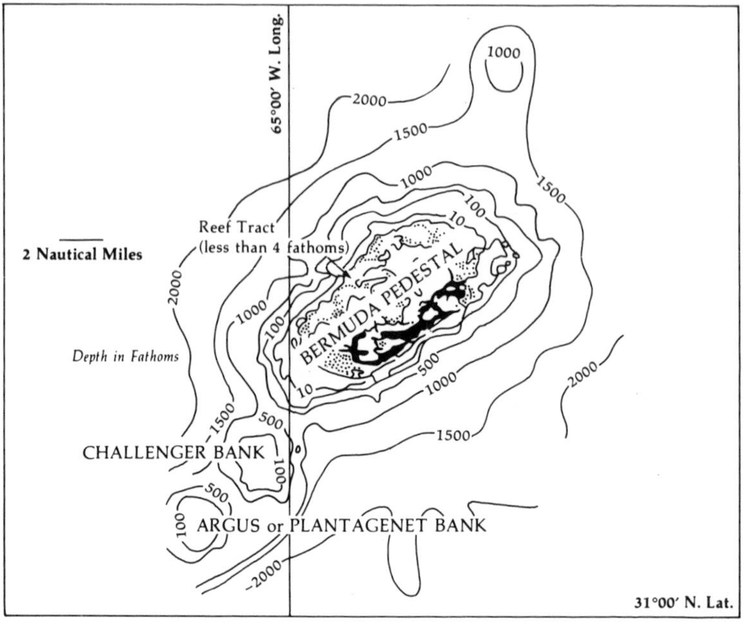

The Bermuda Rise

skeletal remains of the polyps which have nurtured themselves in this excellent environment of warm, shallow, sediment-free water.

Coral is the stony skeletal structure built by any of several marine plants and animals such as the calcareous algae and the coral polyp. Briefly, to explain the process, the polyp extracts calcium carbonate from the sea and deposits it as solid limestone at the polyp's bottom and upwards leading to there being a tube-shaped shell enclosing the polyp. Branching colonies of coral are formed by budding new polyps from the tops of older ones. When a polyp dies, its skeleton remains. Such coral reef builders cannot live more than 91.44 m (300 ft) beneath the sea's surface and corals proper do not live below 45.72 m (150 ft). Furthermore, they cannot survive if the water temperature is less than 18°C (65°F) nor greater than 36°C (96°F); they flourish when the temperature is between 25°C (77°F) and 30°C (86°F). Also, corals prefer moving water

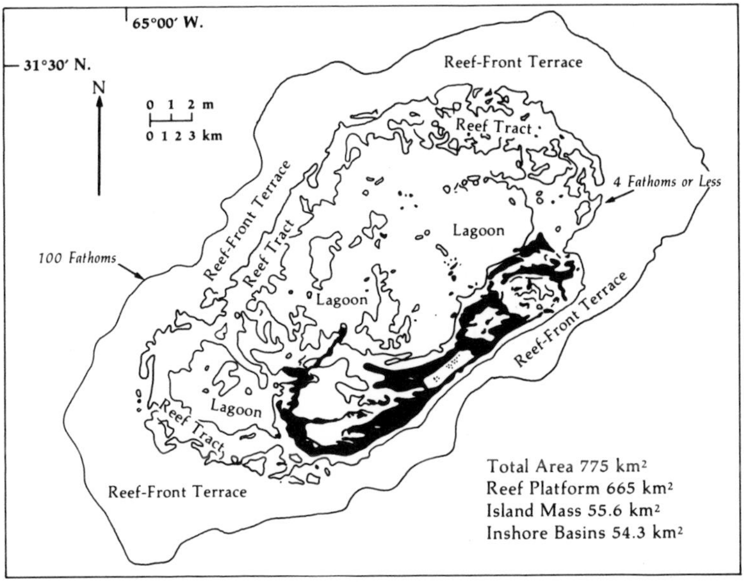

Major Physiographic Provinces of Bermuda
The reef tract and islands enclose a central lagoon that extends to a depth of about 20 metres (after Upchurch, 1970 cited in H. L. Vacher and R. S. Harmon, *Penrose Conference Field Guide to Bermuda Geology* (mimeographed)

because it brings more food and oxygen.

The volcanoes providing the platforms have long been extinct so that, during the last million years, a succession of sea level variations has alternatively exposed and flooded the platforms. These fluctuations have been caused by the phases of the Pleistocene Epoch. During the Glacial Epoch continental ice sheets covered large areas of the northern hemisphere. Alternatively, during the interglacial periods, which lasted hundreds of thousands of years, warm or warmer than present conditions prevailed. The recent epoch of warm conditions is not dissimilar from interglacial ages and, therefore, conditions of the Pleistocene glacial epoch have continued uninterrupted to the present.

When the temperatures were cold, ice caps built up and oceans receded thus revealing the Bermuda Bank as a land surface some ten- to twenty-times greater than it is at present.

Westerly winds and gales deposited fragmented shells and calcareous sand in dune formations on the eastern periphery of the bank. Rain and squalls acted as acidic cementing agents indurating the dunes into what is known as aeolian limestone; aeolian after the Greek god of the winds, Aeolus.

In the following interglacial period, as the ice melted, the Bermuda platform was submerged except for the peripheral dunes, which, as time progressed became vegetated and developed a shallow soil covering. Altogether, it is thought there have been at least four of these changes in sea level and evidence can be found in cuttings through limestone dunes in several parts of the islands. As well, though the soil has sand and lime content, it also owes its richness to climatic conditions and decayed animal and vegetable matter. In 1912, a bore was made in an attempt to find fresh water. The first 109.73 m (360 ft) consisted of limestone, the next 60.96 m (200 ft) of decomposed volcanic calcareous material forming yellowish claylike rock, and finally, to the limit of a 427 m (1,400 ft) boring, only black volcanic rock was found.

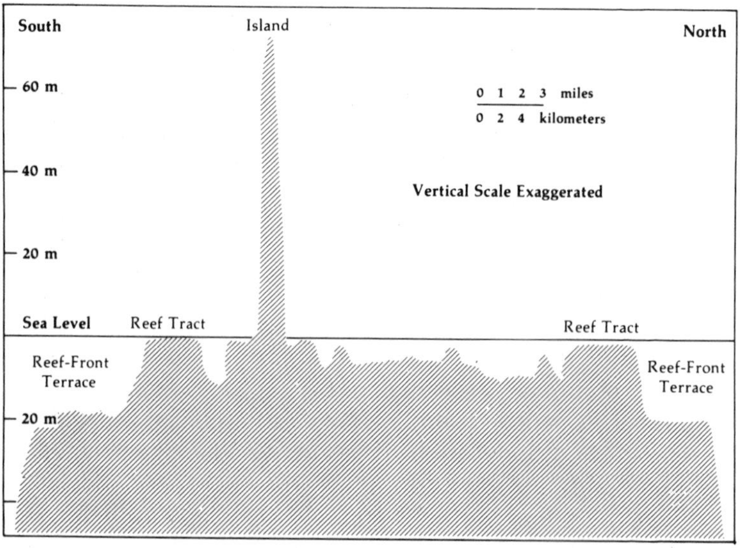

The Bermuda Platform

Relief is generally low but with numerous hills, one of which, Town Hill on the main island, rises to a maximum of 79 m (260 ft). The terrain consists mainly of fertile depressions with marshy areas between the hills. Overall the beautiful scenery, which has entranced so many people, is founded on the interpenetration of sea and land. The many variously shaped islands and rocks, secluded coves, sweeping white beaches, sounds, cliffs, aquamarine and blue water, sea gardens, and submarine flats enhance the magnificence. Finally, to complete this picture, lush green vegetation frames pastel-coloured houses and historic buildings, which the National Trust is so wisely preserving.

CLIMATE AND SOME OTHER NATURAL PHENOMENA

Bermuda's climate is mild, equable, and fairly humid with the average January temperature being 19°C (62.6°F) while the average July temperature is 26°C (78.4°F). Recorded temperature extremes have been 34°C (94°F) and 4°C (39°F). The average daytime temperatures are:

Month	°C	°F
January	20	68
February	19	67
March	20	68
April	22	71
May	24	75
June	27	80
July	29	85
August	30	86
September	29	84
October	26	79
November	23	74
December	21	70

Importantly, the daily temperature range does not exceed 7°C (12°F) and, though the relative humidity usually is more than 70 percent, the sea breezes mitigate against there being excessive physiological discomfort at any time.

To give an indication of recent temperatures, humidity, and rainfall the following table is presented:

	1982	1983	1984
Air temperature (°F)			
Absolute maximum	90 (Jul.)	86 (Sep.)	87 (Aug.)
Absolute minimum	49 (Jan.)	48 (Dec.)	53 (May)*
Mean daily maximum	75	76	75
Mean daily minimum	66	68	69
Mean relative humidity (%)	77	79	77
Annual rainfall (ins.)	60	77	58
Total number of raindays	170	183	154

*An unseasonal occurrence but verified as correct.

The prevailing weather conditions are sometimes described as sub-tropical but, in fact, Bermuda shares the climatic regimes of both the tropical trade-wind belt and the temperate westerly belt. The island's location is in a transitional area between major climatic zones. The Azores-Bermuda high is most well established in July; the atmosphere is heavier than the surrounding air and this leads to there being pleasant weather most of the summer. This is because northern fronts are deflected from penetrating the Bermuda area. The summer southwest breezes prevent extreme heat, and rain squalls may hit one parish but not another. In winter, the warm water of the Gulf Stream is a definite modifier of cold winds from the north – Zuill calls it Bermuda's 'great winter shield'.

Given these conditions, July is the driest month (less than 10.16 cm (4 in) of rain), October the wettest month (over 15.24 cm (6 in) of rain), and August the hottest month (with more rain than July).

Hurricanes

October is not only the wettest month but also the one in which the lowest pressure conditions are experienced. Fronts moving south and east from North America penetrate the Bermuda area. Additionally, tropical depressions often reach the vicinity of the island during October. The most severe hurricanes in recent years (in 1926, 1939, 1947) have all occurred in October. Such storms usually approach from the south-southeast or southwest but, fortunately, by the time they reach the latitude of Bermuda, they have lost much of their intensity. Also, the smallness of Bermuda greatly reduces the probability of the eye of the hurricane passing over the islands.

Hurricanes have been known to approach Bermuda from almost all points on the compass. However, when they do make contact with the islands, the surrounding reefs and islands break the storm waves and protect the coast.

Waterspouts

Waterspouts are tornadoes which occur over water. They are very rare in the Bermuda region but they have been known to hit the islands. Usually on muggy July or August days they can be seen trying to form over the ocean as grey 'tails' dip down from the clouds. If the waterspouts hit land they become tornadoes and, of course, can leave a trail of damage. Bermuda's worst experience was in April 1953 when four of them swept across the islands; a taxi was deposited in the Sound near Harrington Sound Road and its driver was fortunately able to swim ashore. Others came ashore in 1986 and damaged trees and the surroundings of a golf course.

Water Supply

There being no springs, rivers, or streams in Bermuda so inhabitants have traditionally derived their fresh water from the collection and storage of rainwater, and to a limited extent from wells. Rain is collected from the roofs of buildings and stored in tanks under or near houses. Some hilly areas have been cleared of vegetation to base rock then waterproof cemented so as to form catchment areas leading to storage tanks. As well, some hotels have installed saltwater distillation plants. The Government's central distillation plant, established in 1960, was an important development. And, since 1973, 16 million gallons of water per year have been drawn from a freshwater lens under the Pembroke and Devonshire parishes by the Public Works Department. This water is then sold to water trucking companies which, in turn, retail it to consumers in need of supplies.

In 1974, Dr. H. L. Vacher analyzed the groundwater hydrology of Bermuda and provided scientific information on the extent and quantities of water in the underground lenses which are now known to exist over 20 percent of the island in five separate areas. This information led to a Water Resources Act which now protects the use of water lenses by establishing developmental and conservation policies.

However, it is thought that more can be done to deal with the problems and some practical recommendations have been made. For instance, it is reasoned that the groundwater lenses should be protected from over-extraction and contamination, that a single Water Authority should make decisions, that desalination of brackish water and seawater may be required, and that seawater could be used for flushing, providing the saline wastes are not allowed to contaminate the lenses. As well, more economic use of water could be made in homes and hotels; for example, by modifying shower heads to emit less water. It should be noted, however, that the rainwater used for drinking, cooking, and washing is fresh, pure, and quite safe. There are seldom any ill effects or upsets caused by drinking it.

A side effect of the water phenomenon is that water seepage through the limestone, and wind pressure, has led to there being a large number of caves all over the islands. There are the large Crystal and Leamington caves as well as others in which beautiful stalagmite and stalactites are found.

Bermuda Triangle

The Bermuda Triangle is the most notorious of several geographic regions all lying roughly between 30 degrees and 40 degrees of latitude, in which numerous ships and aircraft have vanished without trace. The Triangle covers 3,900,000 sq km (1,500,000 sq miles) between Bermuda, Florida, and Puerto Rico. It is important to realise the sea in this region is very deep and has powerful currents, so these facts may explain the lack of wreckage.

Also, within the area, is what has been known since 1514 as the Sargasso Sea. It is a region of calms, light winds, and clear weather between the trade winds and the westerlies. Generally, it is the ocean equivalent of the Bermuda-Azores high. In it accumulates the Sargassum Weed, a self-supporting olive yellow to golden brown vegetative growth which multiplies as it drifts around the Sargasso Sea. Interestingly, as well, European and North American freshwater eels spawn in the deep warm water before the young larvae spread northwards for two years before ascending the rivers as young elver. The weed also collects modern-day Atlantic floating debris, such as oil, tar, and plastic bottles, which sometimes washes up on Bermuda's shoreline. However, the weed does have utility in Bermuda as it is an excellent fertilizer, after being allowed to rot in a compost heap.

For many years there was no generally satisfactory explanation of the disappearances in the Bermuda Triangle. Kusche, on investigating, found the following reasons for the disappearances being propagated: seaquakes, waterspouts, tidal waves, freak seas, death rays from Atlantis, black holes in space, underwater signalling devices which guided invaders from other planets, UFOs collecting earthlings, time warps, reverse gravity fields, and witchcraft! Generally, a 'vile vortex,' or an anomaly – a place where events and objects do not behave as they normally would. On further inquiry, Kusche found that theorists had sought connections between the lost vessels and their passengers. For example, did the incidents occur at the same time of day, or during eclipses, or during earthquakes, or solar flareups? No theory could account for all or even most of the incidents.

After abandoning the general theory approach Kusche investigated each incident independently and the mystery began to unravel in the following consistent fashion.

1. Once full information was available there were logical explanations for most of the incidents. For example, it was found that the lost *Marine Sulphur Queen* had a weakened structure which probably could not cope with the weather conditions described by the Coast Guard.

2. With few exceptions, the unsolved mysteries have no available information. In several cases entire incidents are fictional.
3. Disappearances occur all over the oceans, and over land. Some losses elsewhere have been credited to the Triangle. Some vessels passed through the Triangle but there is no proof they vanished there.
4. Many incidents were not considered mysteries when they occurred but were made so later by Bermuda Triangle writers.
5. Contrary to the legend, the weather was bad when many of the incidents occurred.
6. Many mishaps happened at night or in the late afternoon which meant that searches could not begin until the next day, and so debris could easily have sunk or dispersed.
7. Many writers on the Triangle have done no original research and have thereby perpetuated the errors and embellishments of earlier accounts.
8. Several writers have withheld information that provided an obvious solution to a disappearance.

In conclusion, Kusche's research serves society well in demonstrating that the legend of the Bermuda Triangle is a manufactured mystery.

VEGETATION AND ANIMAL LIFE

Vegetation

When first discovered the Bermuda Islands were thickly wooded. Citing research on fossil evidence, botanical research, and reports of early settlers, Jickells has provided a composite description of what the islands most probably looked like in terms of plants (and animals; see below). The upland and valley areas were densely forested by cedar and palmetto with an understory of shade- and humus-loving plants. The valleys had hackberry and a wide variety of shrubs, vines, and herbs were found in clearings.

On the coasts were prickly pear, sea ox-eye, Spanish bayonet, sea-side morning glory, sea lavendar together with mangrove and buttonwood trees at the water's edge. Brackish coastal ponds contained marsh samphire, sand spurry, seaside heliotrope, and submerged widgeon grass. Freshwater ponds supported duckweed, mermaid weed, cat-tail, bulrush, and water smartweed.

Over the years some 500 species of introduced plants have become naturalised in Bermuda. That is, they self-propagate in the wild and fifteen of them can be considered pests in that they seriously compete with the native flora, often suppressing or even replacing it. Many of the original upland and valley flora has now been replaced by agricultural crops, gardens, and lawns.

The Bermuda cedar has the capacity to grow in minimal amounts of soil and used to be important in providing timber for building homes and ships. Certainly, the greedy Bermuda Company shipped too large quantities of cedar to England until legislation banned the export of timber in 1657. Unfortunately, two new scale insect pests, the oyster-shell scale and the juniper scale, were accidentally introduced into Bermuda from California in the 1940s. By 1951, approximately 85 percent of the cedars were dead and the remainder were in various stages of defoliation. Spraying had been impractical, and introduced predators were not sufficient for the task. A 1978 study of 424 trees showed that scale is still present but some strains of cedar can tolerate it. Some weakened trees are now recovering as is seen by new growths of bark. The 100,000 lost cedars robbed the islands of an important soil builder, a windbreak, and bird nesting sites. Reforestation with many other species of trees and plants has relatively successfully taken place – notably by planting the Australian casuarina. Also, using the pimento (all-spice), the poincianna, the bougainvillea, the poinsettia, the oleander, hibiscus, the fiddlewood, the Surinam cherry, the Norfolk Island pine, the tamarisk, pittosporum, and palms. Bermuda fruit trees now include Canary Island bananas, poquats, guavas, and a wide variety of citrus. Notable shrubs are the oleander and the hibiscus while a famous flower is the Easter lily, which will be commented on in Chapter 5.

The palmetto provided more varied resources to original

settlers than any other tree; the soft heads of the palm being used as a vegetable, the berries for animal feed or bread, the sap to produce the intoxicant 'bibby,' and the leaves were used for thatching house roofs. In the nineteenth century the fibre from the palmetto tops was used for hats, fans, table mats, baskets, mats, mattresses, and fishing lines. There are fewer of these trees now but, though they grow slowly, they are found in most parts of the island.

There are fifteen other endemic plants of Bermuda including ferns, bushes and shrubs – all can be seen in the 14.56 ha (36 acre) Botanical Gardens. Perhaps the best known is the Bermudiania, an iris-blue flower found in grass all over the islands in the springtime. As well, Bermuda crab grass will be familiar to many in the United States where it is known as St. Augustine grass.

Since the mid-nineteenth century various efforts have been made to preserve vegetation in Bermuda. For example, over the years an experimental station known as McCall's Farm was established (1871–1876), the Agricultural Station opened in 1986, the Nonsuch Island 'living museum' began operations in 1963, the Spittal Pond Nature Reserve was established by the National Trust and the Government in the 1970s, and the Walsingham area (owned by a private trust) aims to preserve the natural features of its area (particularly endemic plants).

Animal Life

Before humans visited the islands several species of turtle visited or bred there and there was a wide variety of birds including the endemic cahow, the Audubon shearwater, tropic-birds, colonies of tern, the vireo, and the following now extinct species: true cranes, two finches, and four rail. Possibly the bluebird and the catbird were present while a wide variety of birds probably visited the islands during migrations, as they do today.

The cahow, also known as the Bermuda petrel, was thought to have been extinct for 285 years when it was rediscovered in 1906. It was rarely seen, however, until 1951 when nesting birds were found on the islands in Castle Roads. There, they were in direct competition with the white-tailed tropic-birds, or 'longtails,' and only one third of the cahow chicks survived. Conservation officers worked hard to help the cahows by constructing artificial nesting burrows and baffles for nest entrances but still the population declined. It was found that DDT contamination was causing the problem, presumably carried from the USA in their oceanic food. Subsequently, DDT and other chlorinated hydrocarbons were banned in the USA and Canada and the cahow's breeding success recovered after 1970. In 1981, there were thirty nesting pairs.

Bermuda Longtail (after Sterrer, 1986)

The longtails, thought by many to be Bermuda's most attractive seabirds, also suffered reductions in numbers because of DDT and urbanization. There are between 3,000 and 4,000 in the islands today but their numbers were thought to be 40 percent higher twenty-five years ago. Between March and October they can be seen sweeping towards their nesting holes in inaccessible cliffs such as on the south shore of Southampton and the Castle Harbour islands.

Other principal birds are the black catbird, the yellow-breasted kiskadee, the European sparrow, the cardinal or redbird, the American crow, the ground dove, and the starling. When the house sparrow was introduced in 1870 the bluebird population began to decline and it was further threatened by the loss of cedars as well as increased urbanization. Furthermore, by the 1950s, starlings competed for food and nestholes while the kiskadee preyed on the bluebirds' eggs and young. In 1957 there were only about 200 starlings on the islands but now there are more than 100,000. Originally introduced to combat the house flies in 1870, the number of sparrows has increased dramatically to the point where there are now believed to be 400,000.

The kiskadee is another example of how biological control can go wrong. It was introduced to Bermuda from Trinidad in 1957 to control the *Anolis* lizards, which were feeding on ladybird beetles. However, the original 200 kiskadees had become 60,000 by 1976 and they were eating insects, soft skinned fruit, crabs, fish, and the eggs and young of the vireo and bluebird.

Bermuda has no native mammals and only one native reptile – the skink, a lizard. The hogs, which were present when the first settlers arrived, had been introduced earlier by humans and had caused considerable ecological damage. After 1612, many animals were introduced to the islands. Dogs were imported at first to hunt hogs, and rats were accidentally introduced from a grain ship. Within two years the rats had multiplied sufficiently to eat all the crops and cause a famine. Cats, poison, traps, and burning forests were used as means to try to eliminate the rats. There was some success but wild cats and dogs were then left roaming the islands in search of food, and this contributed to the reduction in the numbers of seabirds and skinks.

The skink has clawed feet which conservation officers think

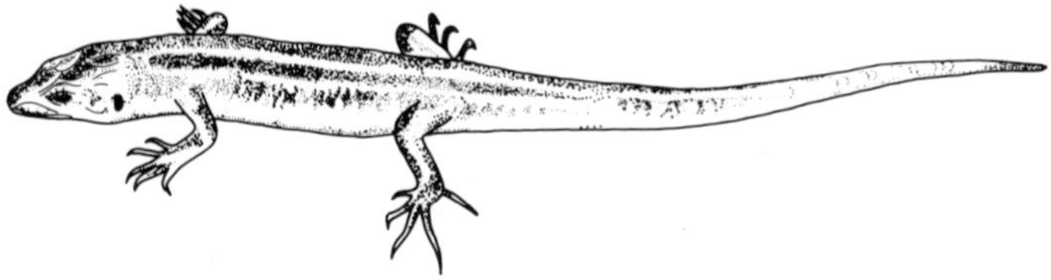

The Skink
Bermuda Rock Lizard (after David B. Wingate, Chart, The Bermuda Press, 1973)

may cause it to get trapped in discarded bottles and cans, thus causing further scarcity of Bermuda's only native land reptile. Skinks rarely enter houses and are generally difficult to find. Other small lizards, which eat flies and insects, are sometimes found in houses. As well, Nathaniel Vesey introduced toads to the islands in 1885 to help control pests. These large, saucer-sized toads live in fields but occasionally wander onto roads. Also, Bermuda has tiny whistling frogs which live in the bark of trees and stone walls. The only poisonous land creature is the rarely found three to four inch centipede which has painful and poisonous pincers. Finally, there are several varieties of spiders, butterflies, moths, houseflies, and mosquitoes – nowadays far fewer of the latter two than there used to be.

The waters surrounding Bermuda are rich in sea life; inshore fish around the reefs and banks with oceanic fish in the deep ocean. Along the coasts are many brightly coloured cowpilots, grey bream, and the silver-green fry. Harder to find are the deep blue angel fish with yellow fins and the colourful parrot fish. In deeper water are rockfish, snapper, hamlet, grouper, mackerel, whipray, and yellowtail. In still deeper water tuna, dolphins, sharks, barracuda, and wahoo may be

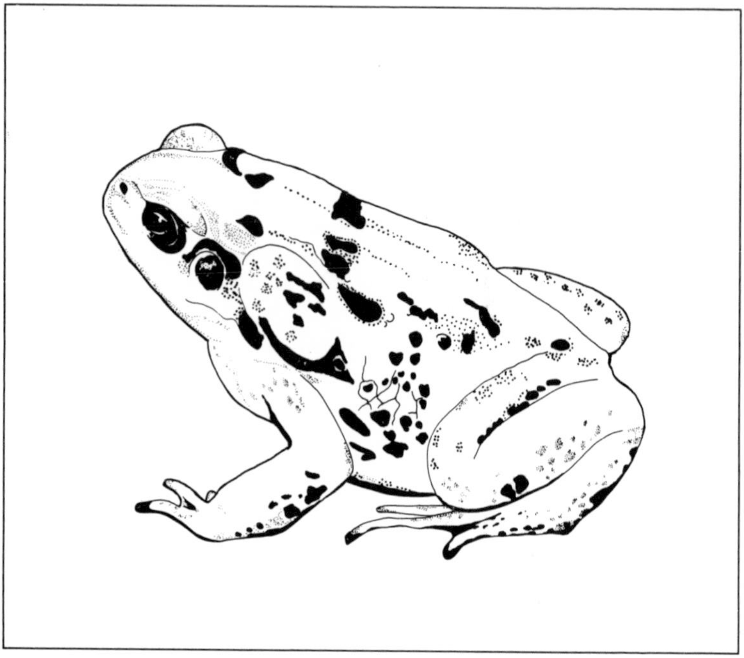

Giant Toad (after Wingate, 1973)

found. Whales pass the islands and occasionally come ashore. Possible swimming hazards are various jellyfish and the Portuguese man-of-war which can give nasty stings. Also, divers should not poke their hands into reef crannies for the Moray eel may give a severe bite if it is disturbed.

The Bermuda Aquarium, established at the Flatts in 1928, has achieved an international reputation and is visited by some 150,000 people each year. It houses twenty-six large fish tanks and a reef tank so as to display over seventy-five species of fish and fifty species of marine invertebrates in a natural setting. A continuous unfiltered water circulation makes it possible to show live coral and seafans, sponges, algae, the curious seahorse, and delicate sea anemonies taken from the reefs around Bermuda. An individualised audio system provides the visitor with interesting background information.

Research into the environmental conditions of Bermuda's

inshore water is carried out by the staff of the Bermuda Biological Station which receives a grant from the Bermuda Government for this purpose. It was established at Ferry Reach, St. George's, in 1932 and is one of the oldest US-founded marine laboratories. Since 1969, it has operated year-round with an increasing variety of programmes related largely to environmental quality, such as the issues of acid rain and the effects of oil on reef-building corals. In fulfilment of its mission the Biostation serves a resident scientific staff and visiting investigators from institutions around the world. During June, July, and August advanced courses in the marine sciences are held with faculty drawn from American and European universities. For those who wish to study these aspects a glossary of Bermudian plants and animals is available in Jickell's 'Plants and Animals' (see Bibliography).

DELICATE BALANCE

Despite the physical advantages described in the earlier sections of this chapter it is also clear that, if Bermuda squandered its scenic attractions, its economic survival would be seriously threatened. The balance is indeed delicate. The Bermuda National Trust is well aware of the dangers and is constantly dealing in small issues which could become large ones. The Trust's environmental committee has created an enduring awareness in the community of the importance of preserving green lands. And, under the editorship of Hayward, Gomez, and Sterrer, the Trust, in collaboration with the Biological Station, published an excellent book of environmental essays which deal with the many interrelated facets of Bermuda's unique environment. As well, the book includes particulars of all the pertinent legislation.

There are also a number of private acts incorporating conservation-oriented bodies for the purpose of environmental conservation. Of course, laws by themselves cannot take care of all the problems and a conservation officer has made recommendations suggesting the need for environmental training programmes for professionals, long-range ecological research, policing the 200-mile limit, and taking legal action against those who damage the environment.

2 GLIMPSES OF THE PAST

Writing about his experiences in Bermuda approximately 130 years ago, a Field Officer (1857) stated that the islands possessed a threefold claim to the attention of Britons – as a colony, a fortress, and a prison. In particular:

> As a *colony*; it claims interest from its remoteness, its primitiveness, the beauty of its scenery, the salubrity of its climate; and also from its having been the earliest colonised of our islands in the western hemisphere.
>
> As a naval and military *fortress*; its value, if not duly appreciated by us will, one day, certainly be so by the Americans.
>
> Lastly, as a *prison*, Bermuda, as the receptacle of our worst convicts, must assuredly possess some degree of interest for every Briton who values the security of his life and property.

These glimpses were taken close to 350 years after Bermuda was first discovered. What led to these observations, and what has occurred in the succeeding one and one-third centuries, is somewhat selectively reviewed in this chapter. Anyone wanting full details of Bermuda's early history is advised to consult the works of Wilkinson. As well, the shorter books by Kennedy, Tucker, and W. S. Zuill are most helpful.

DISCOVERY

Several books and encyclopaedias state precisely when Bermuda was discovered and they are usually close to being correct. However, it does not now seem possible to be absolutely precise.

'La Bermuda' appeared on Martyn's *Legatio Babylonica* in 1511 – the date was established by the text being continued on the back of the map. The discoverer of Bermuda was Juan Bermudez, who, in his ship *La Garza* (the heron) visited the islands in 1515. However, there is nothing to imply that this visit was his first. But, in 1515 he had on board Gonzalo Ferdinandez d'Oviedo y Valdes, a Spanish courtier and later historiographer of the Indies, who later wrote that he had, in 1515, 'sayled above the island Bermuda, otherwise called Garza . . .' He said he intended 'to leave in the island certaine hogs for increase . . .' but 'by reason of contrarie winde, I could not bring my ship no neerer the Island . . .' Wilkinson also cites Herrera (1527) as saying that the island was called Bermuda, or La Garza, 'after the captain who discovered it and of his vessel.'

Clearly, there must be a reason for la Bermuda being on a map before 1515. A likely explanation is that many sailors had passed close to the islands before 1500 – indeed, Christopher Columbus landed in San Salvador in 1492. And, Spanish fleets heading for the Indies left Cadiz sailing southwest to latitude 16 degrees and then due west with the trade winds before going on to Cartegena and elsewhere. On their homeward journeys, with tobacco and sugar cargoes, they sailed through the choppy Bahamas Channel and up the Gulf Stream to about latitude 34 degrees, where, with a southwest wind they passed just north of Bermuda and then east to the Azores. So, since Bermudez was at least known to have had previous commands on the routes in 1500, 1502, and 1503, he probably named the islands 'La Bermuda' on one of those trips. Nevertheless, since the waters around the islands' reefs were so treacherous, they were most likely 'discovered' by other seafarers as well.

Oviedo stated that he could not land the hogs in 1515. However, the Field Officer, writing in 1857 said, 'It is said that when his [Bermudez's] vessel was wrecked, his cargo of hogs swam ashore, where they afterwards greatly multiplied, and became quite wild.' Certainly pigs were early inhabitants and the *Bermuda Report* cites the shrieks and squeals of wild boars left by passing Portuguese and Spanish mariners as giving Bermuda the reputation of being the 'Isle of Devils' – also taking into account the treacherous reefs. The same

Bermuda Report says the islands were discovered in 1503 by Bermudez.

The year 1503 seems a likely one for the following reasons identified by Tucker. She pointed out that in the Chateau de Ramezay in Montreal hangs a map marked '*Carte de la Nouvelle-France, 1690.*' On it are the words, '*Les Isles Bermudes furent decouverte l'an 1503. Les Anglois y ont un establishment depuis l'an 1612.*' Of course, this is not proof, but it is known that Bermuda was certainly discovered before 1511, probably in 1503. Bermudez was a fairly common name at the time, but Herrera's statement is probably accurate so far as the naming is concerned.

HUMAN SETTLEMENT

Spanish explorers led the way westwards and by 1532 America was solidly Spanish from Cape Horn to California, with the exception of Brazil, which the Portuguese had colonized in honour of the Pope's grant. Towards the end of the century reports of the gold and precious metals on Spanish ships reached the ears of adventurous spirits in Europe so that French, Dutch, and then English pirates were pursuing them in the Caribbean.

England was 'too wasted, too worn by religious differences, and too uncertain in her foreign relations, to make any organised efforts at such a distance,' Wilkinson records. And, though Henry VIII was enthusiastically in favour of naval development, England had not regained any stability until Elizabeth had been on the throne for several years. In the decade following 1575, England was prosperous with the people having good health, good crops, and profitable sheep rearing. Importantly, there was an increase in collective enterprises, such as craft and religious guilds, which gradually dealt in larger things and admitted men of means. To some merchant adventurers the Queen gave patents and Sir Walter Raleigh, as one, set out in 1585 to investigate the American coast at what is now North Carolina. He returned with enthusiastic reports so that the Queen thought the place worthy of a name pertaining to her – hence it became

'Virginia' and merchants undertook to develop it, but their task was extremely difficult over the years.

Spain resumed diplomatic relations with England and, in 1604, gave substantial pensions to seven prominent people. With such leverage, Spain tried to get the colonists out of Virginia from where it was thought they could endanger the plate fleet. Wilkinson states the Ambassador bluntly told King James, 'it is desirable your Majesty should command that such a project should be uprooted now, while it can be done so easily.' It was perturbing to Spain to have Protestants with 'their errors and their sects in territory which was Spain's by right.' Nevertheless, the Virginia merchants issued pamphlets extolling the opportunities for the adventurous in their new colony. And a new charter was drawn incorporating the Company of Adventurers and Planters of the City of London for the first Colony of Virginia.

At this point Bermuda's colonial history was about to begin. By May 1609, Sir Thomas Gates, lieutenant-general with absolute command of the new Virginia expedition, was ready to sail with 600 emigrants in seven ships and two pinnaces under the command of the veteran seaman and privateer, Sir George Somers. Somers' fleet left Plymouth on 2 June with the objective of assisting the settlers in Jamestown; and many passengers intended to settle there themselves.

The question of precedence between Gates and Somers arose so they both sailed in the 300-ton flagship *Sea Venture*, which was under the command of Captain Christopher Newport. Also on board were about 150 men, women, and children. When they had been at sea about seven weeks a hurricane struck. Jourdan, a passenger, later wrote 'we were taken with a most sharpe and cruell storme . . .' Wilkinson cites Virginia secretary-elect William Stachey's account of that 14 July 1609 day in full. They lost sight of other ships, it took eight men to hold the steering gear, rain fell in cascades, the wind roared, and goods were thrown overboard. Waist deep in water, people took turns to pump and bail water out . . . 'For foure and twenty houres the storme was fury added to fury . . .' Sir George Somers struggled on the poop for three days and nights until he knew she must soon sink. Suddenly, unexpectedly, he sighted land! He drove the waterlogged *Sea Venture* towards it and soon 'fell in betweene two rockes, where she was fast lodged and locked whereby wee gained not only sufficient time, with the present help of our boate and skiffe to convey our men, women and children . . . to the shore which was three quarter of a mile distant . . . ' It was Friday 28 July – afterwards named Somers' Day. It is believed that the storm later became Shakespeare's *Tempest.* This shipwreck led to deliberate colonization of the Somers' Islands, as they were often called, and they have never been uninhabited ever since. The reef is now called Sea Venture Flat, portraits of Sir George and Lady Somers hang in the Bermuda Historical Society Museum at Par-la-Ville, and a model of the *Sea Venture* rests on City Hall in Hamilton.

Of the other ships that left Plymouth in June, all except one eventually, though in sorry states and with lives lost, reached Virginia. The pinnace *Catch* sank and all hands were lost. So, from these early days, the history of Bermuda and Virginia has been intertwined.

The fortunate survivors of the *Sea Venture* immediately made plans to continue their journey to Virginia. First the *Sea Venture's* longboat was adapted and dispatched to Virginia in search of help. Regrettably, the gallant crew was never seen again. However, in nine months, despite three mutinies, two ships were built – the *Deliverance* and *Patience* – so that the group finally reached Jamestown on 10 May 1610. Sadly, the Jamestown community had been reduced by famine, and Indian attacks, from 500 to 60. The settlers' plight was desperate so Sir George Somers offered to return to Bermuda for plentiful supplies of food – turtles, hogs, and fish. His journey back to Bermuda was in the *Patience* but he was exhausted and died there on 9 November 1610 at the age of fifty-six. The island on which he died is now called St. George's.

When the *Patience* returned to England, three men and the

(*opposite*) Bermuda Tribe Shares. Richard Norwood initially surveyed the islands in 1614 then completed his task during 1616–17. This map is based on his work

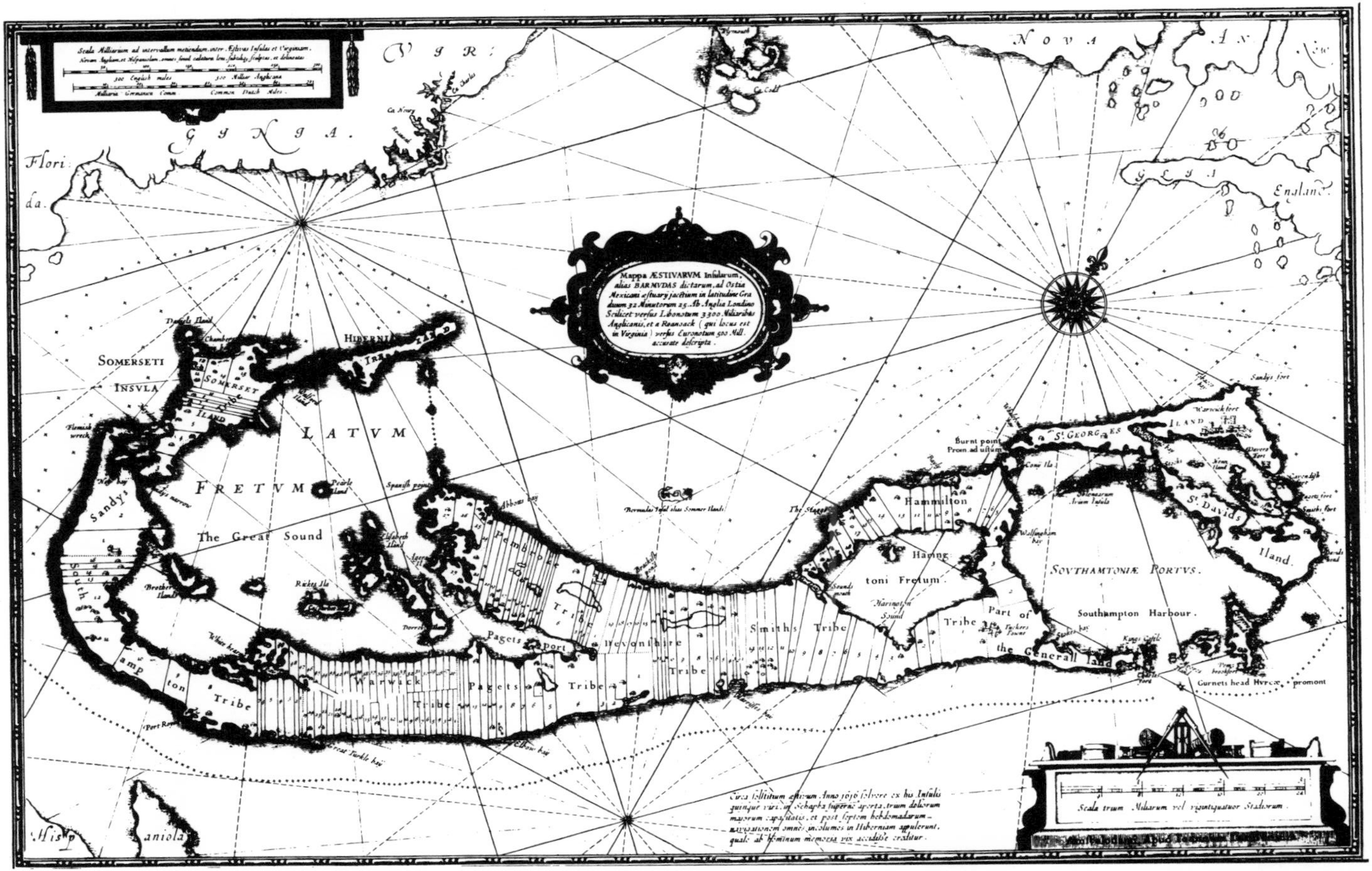
Mappa ÆSTIVARVM Insularum, alias BARMVDAS dictarum, ad Ostia Mexicani æstuary jacētium in latitudine Graduum 32 Minutorum 25. Ab Anglia Londino Scilicet versus Libonotum 3300 Miliaribus Anglicanis, et a Roanoack (qui locus est in Virginia) versus Euronotum 500 Mill. accurate descripta.
Scala Milliarium ad intervallum metiendum inter Æstivas Insulas et Virginiam, Novam Angliam, et Hispaniolam, omnes suaū calcituris locis subjectus sculptas, et delineatas.
300 English miles
300 Milliar Anglicana
Milliaria Germanica Comm.
Common Dutch Miles
Nova
England
Flori
da.
Somerseti Insula
Somerset Iland
Hibernia
Fretum
Latum
The Great Sound
Sandys
South
Brothers Ilands
Flemish wreck
Port Royal
amp ton Tribe
Warwick Tribe
Pagets Tribe
Pagets port
Pembroke Tribe
Devonshire Tribe
Smiths Tribe
Hammilton
Hamngtoni Fretum
Harington Sound
Part of the General land
Tuckers Towne
Southampton Harbour
Southamtoniæ Portus
St. Georges Iland
St. Davids Iland
Burnt point
Prom. ad ustum
Warwick fort
Sandys fort
Smiths fort
Kings Castle
Gurnets head
Spanish point
Abbots bay
Bermudas Isl. alias Sommer Ilands
The Stages
Great Turtle bay
Elbow bay
Peirle Iland
Riches Ila
Elisabeth Iland
Hisp
aniola
Circa solstitium æstivum Anno 1616 solvere ex his Insulis quinque viri in Schapha superne aperta, trium doliorum majorum capacitatis, et post septem hebdomadarum navigationem omnes incolumes in Hiberniam appulerunt, quale ab hominum memoria vix accidisse creditur.
Scala trium Miliarum vel viginti quatuor Stadiorum.

ship's dog remained to hold claim to the islands for England. In 1612 King James I, in the third Virginia charter, extended the jurisdiction of the Virginia Company to include the Summers Islands. Thus the new colony became the property of Sir William Wade, Sir Baptist Hicks, Richard Martin, Richard Chamberlain, Jerome Heyden, Sir Dudley Digges, John Wolstenholme, Robert Offeley, Robert Johnson, George Scott, and George Berkeley. And, on 9 May 1612 the sixty initial permanent settlers were sent out to Bermuda on the *Plough* with Richard Moore, a ship's carpenter as governor. Moore proved to be a wise choice who led the colonists to build wharves and forts to keep the Spanish out. As well, they grew tobacco, corn, wheat, beans, and melons. Perhaps this is an appropriate point to quote Lewis Hughes' *A Letter from the Summer Islands*, which he wrote in 1615. Just as Spain thought Virginia was its property 'by right' so Hughes divinely thought this about Bermuda, 'The King of Spaine had never anything to do heere, and I hope never shall. The King of Kings hath kept these islands from the King of Spain and all other Kings in the world; till now, that it hath pleased his holy Majesty to bestow them upon the King of England.'

It was not, however, found to be expedient to administer two colonies under one company so King James granted the Somers Company a separate charter in 1615. This charter enabled a General Assembly to be called with the power to make laws, provided that the laws were not contrary nor repugnant to the laws of England. With the new charter came a new and energetic governor in Daniel Tucker, who was later immortalised in the Mother Goose rhyme as the one who washed his face in a frying pan. However, it was Daniel Tucker's successor, Nathanial Butler, who introduced the first General Assembly in August 1620 – therefore making

(*opposite*) Aeolian limestone cliffs at Castle Roads with now derelict forts 'guarding peaceful seas'

Devil's Hole. Bermuda's geology is readily available for scrutiny at Crystal Cave and Leamington Caves. Devil's Hole is a former cave which is fed by the sea through a quarter-mile of subterranean passages

Bermuda's Parliament the oldest in the Commonwealth outside Westminster. In Governor Butler's term of office bridges were built to link the main islands and, also, a fort, a church, and a Sessions House were constructed in the then capital town of St. George's. The latter building still stands as the oldest building in Bermuda.

The first negro slaves were taken to Portugal in 1441 and, later, many were sold to Spanish landowners and they soon spread to all Spanish colonies. The first slaves in Bermuda are reported to have been one Indian and one Negro, who were brought there in 1616 to dive for pearls. Within twenty years many more Negroes were brought from the West Indian slave plantations so that slavery became an aspect of life. There were also white slaves who were imported as a result of Cromwell's victories over the Irish. And there were Indian slaves from the English colonies in North America. Not surprisingly there were several slave revolts and people in England began to denounce slavery as vile. In 1772, England's Lord Chief Justice Mansfield initiated a law to make slavery illegal in England where 14,000 coloured people gained their freedom. In Bermuda it took longer.

Meanwhile, in Bermuda, the population in 1669 consisted of 3,615 white people and 2,247 black people. Here were the beginnings of how white and black people would live together for nearly 400 years to become what long-time resident W. S. Zuill can proudly call 'one people'.

Reverting to the 17th century, before concluding this section, the Somers Island Company was decrepit by 1677, and the Adventurers, as then constituted, were derisively denounced by Bermudians as a group of brokers, tobacconists nonconformist ministers, net makers, and retailers of small wares, fit persons for the management of a plantation. So many restrictions were enforced by the private investors who ruled the colony that the islands' economy was being crippled. The colonists petitioned the Crown and the

(*opposite*) Interpenetration of sea and land. In the centre of this picture is a water catchment area and storage tank. The general vegetation and relief are also illustrated

Bermuda (or Somers) Company finally forfeited its charter in 1684. Bermuda became a self-governing colony.

Slightly earlier, in 1668, some adventurous Bermudian seafarers founded a colony of their own on a small island almost 1,000 miles away. They called it Turk's Island because a cactus there looked like the head of a man wearing a fez. Huge salt ponds were built from which the salt was raked from May to October each year. This hot, hard work was a mainstay of the Bermuda economy for more than a century until Bermudians on Turk's Island were imprisoned by the French in 1773 and then, against protests, it became part of the Bahaman colony in 1801.

The Bermuda Company sent Richard Norwood to survey the islands and he produced a chart in 1618 which, apart from showing wreck sites, listed the tribes or parishes which were assigned to, and named after the more distinguished members of the Company. Their eight names are still used but the ninth parish, St. George's, was never considered a tribe.

THE OLD EMPIRE

Daily life for the people was simple and poor. They lived largely off fish (salt cod), potatoes, bananas, bread, and cassava (from the root of the manihot bush which is also the source of tapioca). There were few horses, the 'tribe roads' were very narrow, and inter-island travel was mostly by boat. Masters and slaves tended to be dependent on each other and there are tales of mutual affection as well as of slaves being set free in masters' wills. Sadly, there is also evidence of slaves being flogged by the parish whipper, who became known as the 'jumper' because he made his victims jump. The jail, as mentioned earlier, had an important role. Wilkinson cites a customs officer saying it was a 'nasty dungeon' where the prisoners had 'light neither by day nor night.' And, since the jail was too small to house all the evil doers, recourse was to the stocks where 'the culprits could be seen and rebuked by all who wished to vent their horror or buttress their own sense of turpitude.' The majority of the victims were slaves. The stocks are still maintained for public viewing, and for photographing 'victims,' in the centre of St. George's. The church's attitude to slaves was barely enlightened but there is some further evidence of resistance to slavery developing during the period.

By 1775 Bermuda found itself involved in the consequences of the American Revolution. Known as the American War of Independence, it occurred when the British Colonies along the Atlantic seaboard definitely separated themselves from the mother country.

Wilkinson focusses the issues, so far as Bermuda was concerned, when he states, 'The cry of Bermudians was for food, and that of the Americans for munitions of war.' Since the British blockaded their ports, the colonists placed an embargo on all provisions destined for other parts of the Empire and 'to capture or destroy any vessels arriving thence within their waters.' Bermuda, undecided, held 120 of its ships in harbour and thus paralysed its commerce and endangered its people's lives by the possibility of starvation.

So serious was Bermuda's need for food that the parish representatives met in Paget in April 1775 and, with two dissenting voices, decided to send delegates immediately to the Continental Congress at Philadelphia to beg for food. Though Colonel Henry Tucker was chosen as head of the delegation, he, like many Bermudians, was in a quandary because even members of his own family were divided on whether to be loyal to Britain or to help the colonists. When Tucker led the parochial delegates to Philadelphia on 11 July his Bermuda preservation petition was drafted, according to Wilkinson, 'in such moderate terms that its sentences seemed to alternate between the contending parties and invoke the best attainments of both.' It referred to Bermuda's national liberty and loyalty to the royal family, but it recognized the colonists' suffering and the futility of expecting redress from the British. They turned to the wisdom of the Congress to recognise Bermudians as fellow subjects who were desolate and praying for food. Though they cherished the Americans' cause they regretted that their numerical insignificance prevented them from being able to give reciprocal help to their continental brethren. They made verbal mention of the fact that some royal powder was stored in Bermuda so, not surprisingly, within four days the Congress resolved that any vessel the Bermudians should send north with munitions of war would not return to the island empty. But no definite commitment was made by either side.

Meanwhile, the Americans were vigorously searching for powder, and Commander-in-Chief George Washington said, 'No quantity of powder, however small, is beneath notice.' He wrote a letter for an emissary to deliver in Bermuda, if necessary, in which he asked for sympathy and then tactfully suggested that Bermudians might avail themselves of the opportunity to help the Americans secure the powder in return for provisions. However, the document was never presented. Even so, during the still night of 14 August 1775 'several dozen men scurried noiselessly over the northern hill to the powder magazine' which was quite close to Government House in St. George's on land owned by Governor George Bruere. The men pierced the vaulted roof, lowered a man in, unbolted the door, quietly extracted 100 barrels of powder, and trundled them down the hill to waiting boats which quickly sailed miles off shore in the darkness! Bruere, stunned and in a frenzy when he found out, offered rewards for information leading to the conviction of the culprits, but they were never caught. The powder reached the continental armies and, since the Congress anticipated a long war against George III, it authorized the shipment of a year's provisions to Bermuda on 22 November 1775.

Bermudians also supplied salt for the Americans from Turk's Island and, over the war years, became increasingly dependent on American corn and other provisions. However, Bermuda also received victuals from Britain and, in the end, largely remained loyal to the Crown. Bermuda privateers raided American shipping, and some of Bermuda's ships were captured by the American revolutionaries who threatened invasion of the island.

At last, on 19 October 1781 the Earl of Cornwallis and his 7,000 hard-pressed British and German troops capitulated and the last phase of the ill-fated but momentous war came to an end. Wilkinson cites George III as recognizing that the war left a terrible rift in 'a once respectable Empire.' However, nowhere was peace more welcome than in Bermuda where trading was able to resume.

Finally here, *The Bermuda Gazette and Weekly Advertiser*, the first newspaper, was started in 1784; it was the forerunner of the current daily *The Royal Gazette*. And, the plan to move the seat of government to Hamilton was begun by Governor Henry Hamilton who went to Bermuda in 1788 – the building of Hamilton began in 1792 and it became the capital in 1815.

SIGNIFICANT SOCIAL CHANGES

Dockyard

During the 1800s, important social changes occurred in Bermuda. Prior to 1800 Britain recognized the value of having a strong naval fortress in the western hemisphere to help guard its Empire. It was in 1810, however, that construction work began on the Naval Dockyard at Ireland Island, the westernmost island of the Bermudas and one of the most neglected. British taxpayers' money flowed into Bermuda and provided jobs for local people long after the building work was completed. Artificers from England were sent out to direct slave labourers and then, later, more than 1,600 convicts were shipped from Britain and used for the work. The prisoners were housed in hulks off St. George's, off Ireland Island, and in buildings on Boaz Island. Before the penal exile system was abolished in 1863, some 9,000 convicts served parts of their sentences in Bermuda. Approximately 2,000 of them died in Bermuda, largely as victims of yellow fever epidemics. Finally, Bermuda had a mighty fortress which became the Royal Navy's headquarters for the American and West Indies Squadron. The Imperial Dockyard, with the largest floating dock in the world, was a tremendous boon to Bermuda's economy throughout the nineteenth century – it actually remained open until 1951 and was referred to by many as 'the Gibraltar of the west.'

War of 1812

The American Congress sanctioned the war on England in June 1812, as Wilkinson explains, 'for free trade and sailors' rights', while the British press thought President Madison had opened hostilities 'on the only power which was upholding the liberties of Europe and the world.' Tucker interprets the United States' purpose to be a mere pretext to seize Canada while Britain was preoccupied in a struggle with France. She relates how firmly Bermudians stood by the mother country in this three-year war despite the hardships it brought them. There was a revival of privateering and, despite the enemy capturing forty of Bermuda's vessels, the islanders captured forty-three foreign-built ships to give them a merchant marine of more than seventy vessels by the end of the war.

This was another occasion for the Franco-American alliance to lay plans for the capture of Bermuda. However, because of other priorities, the plan was shelved. There were many actions and losses on both sides until the American and British Commissioners met in Ghent to try to work out the conditions of peace. Meanwhile, the British *Royal Oak* and her fleet carrying field regiments assembled in Bermuda in preparation for an attack on Washington. Bermudian Joseph N. Hayward piloted the fleet through difficult North Rock Passage and it went on to sack and burn the White House and many other buildings. Though often fashionable nowadays to call this vandalism, Tucker reasons it to be a courageous act of war brought about by the American looting of York (now Toronto). There were some other battles until, finally, the Treaty of Ghent was signed on Christmas Eve 1814 and hostilities ceased as soon as the news of it reached the warring factions.

The End of Slavery

In the early 1830s there were about 10,000 people in Bermuda of whom half were black and half were white. Of the black people only 740 were free. Thus, a great social change watershed was reached in England on 29 August 1833 when the Abolition of Slavery Law was passed. It made the holding of slaves in any British possession illegal, though it did provide for there being the possibility of a six-year apprenticeship period. But, in February 1834 Thomas Butterfield introduced the Emancipation Bill in the Bermuda Assembly, without any apprenticeship proviso, to come into effect on 1 August 1834. On that day, all the slaves in Bermuda were to be set free unconditionally. When that great Friday came to Bermuda, churches all held appropriate services and there were marches full of enthusiasm and joy. The British allowed for £20 million to be equitably distributed in the colonies, and then to individual slave owners, as compensation for losing their slaves. The appraisers valued Bermuda slaves at £174,463; there being disproportionate payments in some colonies. By September 1835, £50,000 had been paid to Bermuda but some settlements took ten years to complete. Generally, though, the attitude of the former owners for the compensation was one of gratitude.

In contrast to the Bermuda situation, it would be another thirty years before slavery was abolished in the United States.

American Civil War

The American Civil War was a conflict lasting four years between the United States Federal Government and eleven southern states that asserted their right to leave the Union.

One month after the outbreak of the war, Queen Victoria forbade her subjects to be involved. Tucker cites her as prohibiting 'all British subjects from taking part, or participating in any way whatsoever, either by land or sea, in the existing hostilities between the United States and the Confederate States.' But despite this wise edict, the four-year war changed the pattern of life in Bermuda, bringing violence, excitement, and a great wave of false prosperity. Generally, Bermudian's sympathies lay with the southern states, with whose people they had long connections, so they helped the Confederate cause by running the Federal blockade. They supplied the South with food and munitions, then brought back bales of cotton for transhipment to Britain. Tucker describes the streets of St. George's during this period as being crowded with 'spies, adventurers, secessionists, captains, and crews from the ports of many countries . . . Money flowed like water and the grog shops did a roaring trade.' Many ships were seized or sunk by US Federal cruisers but many people made fortunes. Though the US Navy attempted to blockade

St. George's harbour, it desisted after sharp protests from the British authorities. At the end of the bustling wartime trade, there was a bonus of £27,000 in the Bermuda Treasury.

Portuguese Settlers

Prior to, and after the American Civil War, Portuguese farm workers began to arrive in Bermuda from Madeira and the Azores. They concentrated on growing potatoes, onions, and tomatoes for export to the United States at those chilly times of the year when it was difficult to grow vegetables there. Though they were migrant workers initially, many later settled in Bermuda and Tucker characterises them by 'their thrift, agricultural skill, exemplary conduct and an unequalled tempo of hard work.' Currently, they are interested in, and involved with, the public affairs of Bermuda as well as retaining their agricultural heritage.

Sail to Steam

It was also during the nineteenth century that the great seafaring transition from sail to steam took place. The British Government granted a charter to a group of financiers in 1839 who were interested in the West Indies. They established the Royal Mail Steam and Pacquet Company whose ships went to Barbados then Grenada before branching throughout the Caribbean. One line went westwards to Belize, Vera Cruz, Tampico, Havana, and Nassau once a month. After leaving Nassau the ships would travel to Bermuda and coal, if necessary, before returning to England. The ships carried 'seventy passengers in comfort and splendour' taking fifteen days to reach Plymouth. Tucker describes how Bermudians were struck by 'terror and amazement' when they first saw the Royal Mail Line's SS *Thames* in 1842. Overall though, the advent of steam spurred Bermudians to build five of their fastest and most beautiful clipper ships between 1853 and 1864.

Miscellaneous Developments

Numerous other social changes occurred during the 1800s. The Bermuda Library was founded in 1839, the first bank was established in 1858, tennis was introduced from Britain in 1873, St. David's Lighthouse began to shine in 1879, the first Bermuda dinghy races were held in 1882, three large schools (Saltus Grammar School, Mount St. Agnes Academy, and Bermuda High School for Girls) were founded between 1888 and 1893, while the first telephone and cable service was introduced between 1887 and 1890. Finally, it dawned on Bermudians that hospitality to visitors could be an attractive industry and a pleasant way of life – the great tourist industry was born.

THE GREAT WARS

The twentieth century, so far, has been one which has seen significant changes in Bermuda's politics, economy, tourism, education, the arts, and sports. These concerns are dealt with, and made current, in succeeding chapters. This section deals with Bermuda's connections with some of this century's wars and, to a limited extent, to the aftermath of them.

Boer War

The Boer War, fought in South Africa between the Boers and the British, just after the turn of the century, widened the experience of some Bermudians and helped to strengthen Bermuda's ties with the Caribbean. It was not that the Bermuda garrison fought in South Africa but it stemmed from the fact that thousands of Boer prisoners were sent to the islands to be guarded. The British garrison was then given the task of guarding the Boers while the supplementary West India Regiment's duty was to defend the islands. Apart from becoming acquainted with West Indians, many Bermudians felt sorry for the Boers and helped them. It seems that many of the Boers were excellent carvers and numerous of their cedar souvenirs can still be found in Bermuda.

World War I

In the years leading up to the 1914–18 War, Bermuda's importance as a naval base diminished somewhat as attention centred on Europe. Four naval squadrons were abolished,

Bermuda lost its admiral, and the Fourth Cruiser Squadron took over a large area, with a captain in charge. However, early in 1914, trouble in the Caribbean led to the Fourth Cruiser Squadron being semi-permanently based in Bermuda under the command of Rear-Admiral Sir Christopher Cradock. Sadly, shortly after the outbreak of the war on 14 August 1914, Cradock and all the men on the *Monmouth* and the *Good Hope* lost their lives in a battle against the powerful German cruisers *Scharnhorst* and *Gneisenau*, which were under the command of Vice-Admiral Maximilian Reichsgraf von Spee. Cradock's basic tasks were to help blockade German ships in American ports to stop them returning home, and to stop German warships attacking allied vessels. Thus, it was while following the German ships, which it was thought might come through the Panama Canal from the Pacific, that the British sailors lost their lives off Chile on 10 October 1914. The British sailors had made many friends while ashore in Bermuda, and now, Cradock Road on Ireland Island commemorates their bravery. Not long afterwards, Admiral von Spee went down with his ships at the hands of British Admiral F.C.D. Sturdee in the Battle of the Falkland Islands.

On land, the white Bermuda Volunteer Rifle Corps (BVRC) was mobilized to assist the Lincolnshire Regiment by manning outports and guarding vital points. At the same time the black Bermuda Militia Artillery (BMA) was trained as a coastal defence corps. However, it was not long before both units were on active duty in France; the BVRC with the Lincolnshire Regiment and the BMA (renamed the Bermuda Contingent of the Royal Garrison Artillery) joined the Royal Artillery and worked in dangerous ammunition dumps just behind the front lines. More than 360 Bermudians went overseas and more than forty did not return. As well, other Bermudians served in other branches of British, Empire, and US forces.

Throughout the war the well-protected Bermuda Dockyard was able to carry out most valuable repair work. Of course, regular steamship services were interrupted and, for a while, Bermuda relied on the old HMS *Charybdis* to bring her supplies. After the United States declared war on Germany in

April 1917, the Bermuda base became busier – especially, when the Americans formally set up Base 24 in the Great Sound at Morgan and Tucker's Islands. This was a time when close links were established between the USA and Bermuda for, not only was the fleet using Bermuda as a base, the Americans were bringing many of Bermuda's food supplies.

World War II

During the very early part of the war, Bermuda tried to keep the tourist industry going but, soon, it was in what Tucker called a 'tail spin' and Hannan referred to as 'hibernation'. The streets of Bermuda were empty, necessities of life rationed, mail frequently cut off, and unemployment faced many people. Some relief came when the British set up a mail censorship station in Bermuda and posted 1,500 people there to intercept Atlantic mail. The censors lived in the abandoned Princess and Bermudiana hotels and provided valuable services for the war effort. Among the censors were large numbers of expert linguists so that, overall, they led to the discovery of several German spies in the United States.

Perhaps the most significant development in Bermuda was what Tucker calls 'the sacrifice of one-tenth of Bermuda's whole area, given up for defence bases to the United States of America.' Prime Minister Winston Churchill and President Franklin Roosevelt reached agreement on 3 September 1940 that the United States should acquire ninety-nine-year leases on bases in Bermuda, Newfoundland, the Bahamas, Jamaica, Antigua, St. Lucia, Trinidad, and British Guiana. The Bermuda and Newfoundland bases were given to the United States while the others were in exchange for fifty old US Navy destroyers which were desperately needed for anti-submarine battle duty; some of it very close to Bermuda. In fact, the British Treasury paid for the privately owned Bermuda land in accordance with the requirements of the Lands Acquisition Act.

Though construction workers crowded into Bermuda the whole enterprise was met with mixed feelings until, on 7 December 1941, the Japanese attacked Pearl Harbour and the USA was in the war. The British naval officers yielded responsibility and pride of place to the Americans though they carefully taught the Americans the local mores. By the close of the war the Americans had added 198.70 ha (491 acres) to Bermuda by dredging shoal waters, they had built an invaluable civil airport, and the American personnel became what Tucker calls 'a welcome part of the Bermuda scene, and whose spending helps the local economy.'

As in World War I, Bermudian young men volunteered bravely to serve overseas. The BVRC (later to become the Bermuda Rifles) joined the Lincolnshire Regiment again and served in France while the BMA, and its wartime offspring the Bermuda Militia Infantry, became part of the Caribbean Regiment and fought in the Middle East. All told, 184 Bermudians served abroad of whom thirty-seven lost their lives and one was reported missing. As well, others joined the RAF and the Royal Canadian Air Force in whose service they saw action in many theatres of war. As an afternote, both Bermuda's military units were reorganised in 1951 then amalgamated in 1965 to become the present Bermuda Regiment – an important step forward in the integration of the races.

Zuill comments that, compared with many other countries, Bermuda scarcely suffered at home. There were shortages, sorrows, and worries but the war produced 'a feeling of togetherness' despite its horror and devastation abroad.

ASSASSINATION AND AFTERMATH

The vast majority of people in Bermuda, and their elected political leaders of both parties, have striven diligently to build racial harmony and, on the whole, they have been successful. Events in the 1970s, however, indicate that the task is not completed – just as it is not completed in many other parts of the world. Nevertheless, considering Bermuda's location, size, history, and tourist-driven economy, it simply cannot survive if overt conflict lasts for even fairly short periods of time. Assassinations in 1973 had an aftermath in 1977 which prompted *The Royal Gazette* to say the troubles had 'scorched the national spirit . . .' and, 'it is possible to destroy

Bermuda, and we are very close.' On the same vein, Butland commented, 'It [Bermuda] cannot withstand many tremors of the intensity of 1977, and a major community earthquake could convert a promising future into the ruins of paradise lost.'

World attention was centred on Bermuda after Sir Richard Sharples, Governor and Commander-in-Chief of Bermuda, was assassinated on 10 March 1973. Sir Richard was educated at Eton, the Royal Military College, Sandhurst, and had been an officer in the Welsh Guards with active service during the War of 1939–45 in France, Italy, and the Far East. On leaving the army he was a MP(c) representing the Sutton and Cheam constituency from 1954–72. When he was Minister of State at the Home Office he had to visit Northern Ireland at the time of the 1970 riots. Then, his home and London flat were guarded 24-hours a day. At that time, trouble was expected but it certainly was not when he became Governor of Bermuda in October 1972. And, indeed, Tucker reports that he and Lady Pamela Sharples 'reached out in friendship and sympathy to every segment of the population, making an indelible impression full of hope and promise . . . [his] ambition was to be "The People's Governor".'

On the evening of 10 March 1973 Sir Richard, and his aide-de-camp, Captain Hugh Sayers, attended an informal dinner party at Government House after which, as was their custom, they took the Governor's Great Dane, Horsa, for a stroll in the House's bushy gardens. There, the peaceful scene was shattered when the Governor, his aide, and the dog were all shot dead.

The Times (London, 12 March) reported that 'the shootings have caused consternation in this sunny resort island . . . [for] the incident comes almost exactly six months after Mr. George Duckett, the Commissioner of Police was shot dead.' The speculation was that the two sets of killings were linked but, at the time, there was no proof. The *Bermuda Official Gazette* (17 March, 1973) reported that in accordance with the Defence Act, 1965, Acting Governor I. A. C. Kinnear embodied the Bermuda Regiment as from 0900 on 11 March 1973. Then, applying the powers given to him in the Police

Act, 1951 he called the Reserve Constabulary out for general duty as from 0800 on 13 March 1973. The Emergency Powers Act, 1963 was invoked on 11 March 1973 and again for further periods of fourteen days on 24 March 1973 and 7 April 1973. In the state of emergency, two Scotland Yard detectives were immediately flown from London at the request of the Bermuda Government. Sea and airports were sealed, road-blocks were set up, houses were searched, and people were questioned, but there was nothing definite to report. The British Foreign Office stated that it had no knowledge of any political motive for the killings. And, it was assumed that with the new constitution (see Chapter 4) and the first black Government leader, Sir Edward Richards, Bermuda would enjoy political calm.

The whole affair was discussed in the British House of Commons and, speaking in the Bermuda House of Assembly, Sir Edward Richards told the House that, 'this terrible, senseless killing of Sir Richard and his aide-de-camp has shocked and stunned us all, in this House, in Bermuda and, indeed, throughout the world.' *The Times* (13 March 1973) reported that outside in the sunshine there was little sign of crisis, with whites and blacks going about their business as normal in the picturesque town. However, the paper went on to say that many people in Bermuda wondered whether or not a black group was behind the killings; but there was no public evidence.

By 14 March 1973, Detective Chief Superintendent Bill Wright of Scotland Yard had called in all Bermuda's 800 licensed guns to the police for ballistics tests. He said the weapon appeared to be a handgun but he did not know whether it was the work of a crank or a professional. Fifty people had been questioned and six, who were associated with a militant black movement, had been detained under the emergency regulations. Lady Sharples said the Governor had been in favour of independence for Bermuda and that they had been happy with the way Bermudians had received them with spontaneity and friendship. She commented, 'I can only think this is temporary madness.'

Aftermath

The climax of the aftermath of Governor Sharples' death came in the early days of December 1977.

Erskine Burrows had been sentenced to death on 6 July 1976 having been found guilty of murdering Police Commissioner Duckett in December 1972, and later of murdering Governor Sharples and Captain Sayers. Initially, Ladry Winfield Tacklyn was tried separately on the same murder charges but was acquitted. But, in November 1976, both Burrows and Tacklyn were found guilty of murdering two supermarket managers in April 1973, and thus Tacklyn was also sentenced to death. Tacklyn appealed against the verdict to the Bermuda Court of Appeal but the Court rejected his plea in April 1977. Following this rejection, the Bermuda Prerogative of Mercy Committee advised that neither Burrows nor Tacklyn should be reprieved and the then Acting Governor decided to accept the Committee's advice. An application to the Privy Council for special leave to appeal was dismissed on 6 October 1977. Meanwhile, a petition for clemency to Her Majesty the Queen on behalf of both men was signed by about 6,000 people.

Dr. David Owen, British Secretary of State for Foreign and Commonwealth Affairs, made a statement in the House in which he explained that he had referred the matter to the new Governor, who considered the issues raised in the petition. Again the Prerogative of Mercy Committee advised against reprieves so the Governor saw no grounds for changing the earlier decision of the Acting Governor. Then, Dr. Owen went on, he had consulted former Colonial Secretary Mr. Arthur Creech-Jones' 1947 policy which had been followed for thirty years, had satisfied himself that there were no grounds for believing that there had been a miscarriage of justice, and therefore he said he had no alternative but to advise Her Majesty not to intervene. An announcement to this effect was made on 25 November and the date for the executions was set for 2 December. The Governor, who is responsible to the British Government for Bermuda's internal security, Dr. Owen explained to the House, consulted the Premier and Bermuda Ministers, who are responsible for all other aspects of internal affairs, on whether a stay of execution should be granted because of possible reactions to the executions. They advised the Governor that racial harmony, respect for law and order, and the security situation would suffer more if a stay of execution was granted.

Then on 1 December Tacklyn's last minute appeal to the Supreme Court was rejected on the grounds that the Court had no jurisdiction in the matter. In Britain, some Labour MPs sought a meeting with Dr. Owen to plead for clemency, and the Speaker disallowed a motion for an emergency debate in the Commons. Thus, with all avenues of appeal closed, the two black men were hanged on the morning of 2 December 1977, in the Casemates prison on Ireland Island – the first such executions for more than thirty years.

On the night before the executions a demonstration occurred outside the Supreme Court building which had to be broken up by police using tear gas. A number of buildings were burned, possibly through arson, including a hotel in which three people died. The Governor, Sir Peter Ramsbottom, announced a state of emergency on 2 December and the Bermuda Regiment was embodied between 2 December and 17 December. The emergency measures and dawn-to-dusk curfew had some initial calming effect on 2 December but soon groups of youths caused extensive damage to property using home-made fire bombs and other missiles. Fortunately, there was no serious personal injury.

On 3 December the entire police force had to be called out to deal with a group of about 500 youths which had assembled with the intention of mounting further attacks on property. The Governor considered that the police and the Bermuda Regiment would not be able to contain the situation much longer and he asked for reinforcements from Britain. To meet the request as rapidly as possible a small contingent of eighty men from the Belize garrison was dispatched to Bermuda. They were then joined by a 200-strong company of the Royal Regiment of Fusiliers from Britain, whose members were to remain as unobtrusive as possible in Bermuda.

When *The Times*' and other reporters tried to question the black youths about their motives they said the black murderers would not have been hanged if their victims had not been white and had not included the Governor and the Commissioner. Also, they regarded the Government as unrepresentative of the protesters – even though it had white and black members.

On 3 December, after attacking cars, and pulling a white man off his motorcycle in the 'no-go' area of Court Street, the youth groups were partially dispersed by police wearing helmets and carrying riot shields. As well, the police were aided by heavy rain which lasted some five hours from 5:30 pm. Some Bermuda Government members thought the only way to deal with the rioters was 'to use real force and get on top of all this, or Bermuda will break up.' A helpful moderating appeal was made by Mrs. Lois Browne-Evans, Leader of the opposition Progressive Labour Party, who asked the people to end the violence. Of course the economic dysfunctional consequences began to occur immediately as hundreds of Americans cut short, or cancelled, their holidays – and they were reported as saying, there were plenty of other warm weather resorts vying for their custom.

By 5 December Premier David Gibbons had partially lifted the curfew and said that most of the troops would be leaving Bermuda within days. He also described the rioting as mild 'compared with Washington or Notting Hill' and gave facts on the progress being made towards racial equality in Bermuda. On 7 December *The Times* reported another quiet night and further lifting of the curfew.

More broadly, *The Times* (6 December) debated 'The last stages before independence' in colonies and the difficulties caused by divided responsibilities. Dr. Owen received criticism from politicians in Britain for allowing the executions when they would not have been carried out in Britain. As well, *The Times* (7 December) described how angry Mr. David Gibbons, Bermuda's Premier, was with Dr. Owen's statement in the Commons to the effect that he was only doing what the Government of Bermuda wanted when he did not grant reprieves. Mr. Gibbons agreed that Dr. Owen correctly indicated what the Bermuda Government had said on the issue but that 'He [Dr. Owen] could have granted a reprieve on behalf of the Queen at any time and we would be obliged to take cognizance of that.'

RECENT EVENTS

Bermuda entered the 1980s optimistically with rapidly growing tourism and international companies' activities at all-time highs. The islands, by then, had a good reputation for political and economic stability so the Government and private sector viewed their future challenges with enthusiasm.

Nevertheless, the first five years of the decade brought a number of crises – industrial confrontations, housing shortages, environmental concerns at home and abroad, and a period of economic recession. Despite these difficulties, Bermuda recorded one of its most productive periods in recent history and a number of important projects were completed.

In legislation, Bermuda got its first Human Rights Act and a Human Rights Commission; new health and safety at work laws, and the alco-analyser to help reduce the number of alcohol-related traffic accidents. Discussion papers were presented on labour relations, youth, and on the problems posed by private cars and road traffic. Government and private capital development was prolific and, for the first time, private roads were given official names and numbers were assigned to each dwelling. As in the remainder of the world, computer technology swept into businesses, government, and the schools. Similarly, the survey method of gathering information was used increasingly by the Government, political parties, schools, and consultants. Also, an extensive population census was completed in 1980.

Political

The current political structure is dealt with more fully in Chapter 4 but, briefly here, recent developments are noted. Two years after the 1980 general election in which the Progressive Labour Party (PLP) gained four seats, Bermuda saw a change in its leadership. In January 1982, the Hon. Sir David Gibbons (as he is now titled) stepped down as Premier of Bermuda and was replaced by the Hon. John W. D. Swan who had defeated Dr. the Hon. Clarence James in an election for the United Bermuda Party (UBP) leadership. On the new Premier's popularity, a general election was held in February 1983 and the UBP regained four seats thus giving it twenty-six seats overall against the fourteen held by the PLP.

Government House also saw some changes in the early 1980s. Sir Peter Ramsbottom completed the term of his appointment in December 1980 and was succeeded by Sir Richard Posnett who served until February 1983. He was replaced in July 1983 by Viscount Dunrossil, a former post-war RAF pilot and career diplomat.

The 1981 Strike

One of Bermuda's worst industrial confrontations occurred in April–May 1981 when about 1,200 Government and hospital industrial employees went on strike and thousands of other workers joined them in sympathy. Within a week the islands were at a virtual standstill, and the number of tourists dropped dramatically from 12,000 to 2,000. The dispute stemmed from the inability of the Bermuda Industrial Union (BIU) to reach agreements with the Bermuda Government and the Bermuda Hospitals' Board on new two-year collective agreements for weekly-paid industrial workers. These included garbage collectors, ferry boat crews, bus drivers, and non-medical hospital staff.

There were ugly scenes at the airport as picketing strikers blocked the entry road so that tourists were forced to carry their own bags to and from the terminal building. Yet despite the chaos – and the nearest Bermuda has ever been to a general strike – there was no violence. However, during the tensest period, Governor Posnett embodied the Bermuda Regiment and called up the Reserve Constabulary. Fortunately, negotiations resumed in early May and a mutually acceptable agreement was finally signed in July. Nevertheless, millions of dollars were lost to the economy and that fact, together with the attendant problems, illustrate how almost any dispute can escalate if there is no ready mechanism to arrive at the least painful resolution.

Hospital Commission of Inquiry

After five persons died in 1982 following visits to the Emergency Department of King Edward VII Memorial Hospital, the hospital came in for considerable public criticism. The patients' families recommended that an independent commission of inquiry be established and the Bermuda Hospitals' Board welcomed the suggestion so that public confidence in the hospital could be restored. The Governor appointed a Commission which held hearings between 18–29 October 1982. The final report noted that the hospital was well staffed, well equipped, and well maintained for one of its character. However, the Commission found that improved communications were needed between staff, patients, and the patients' relatives. Also, that the hospital's services should be extended so as to accommodate, and treat separately, emergency and urgent ambulatory care cases.

Subsequently, the hospital has responded responsibly to the Commission's recommendations. An experienced specialist in Emergency Medicine was recruited from Canada and a highly qualified nurse was assigned to the waiting room as Triage Officer to assess the patients' conditions and keep them informed while waiting. As well, an ombudsman was appointed with a view to enhance communications between patients and the hospital. It was also agreed that a study would be undertaken to assess the need for physical expansion of the facilities.

Alcohol and Drugs Commission

In the late 1970s and early 1980s there was public concern in Bermuda about the rising use and misuse of illicit drugs and alcohol. After consultations with several ministries in 1983, Premier Swan appointed Dr. David Archibald, from Canada, to be a one-man Royal Commission to delve into the issues.

By March 1985, six reports had been completed and it was clear that Bermuda has serious problems with illicit drugs and alcohol which are affecting all segments of society. The reports include recommendations for policies and programmes to be established so that the difficulties can be lessened. In fact, Dr. Archibald felt that Bermuda was one of the very few countries in the world that could be successful in reducing such problems to a tolerable level.

Housing Shortage

Though there had been a housing shortage in the late 1970s the situation was worse at the beginning of the 1980s. The Government suddenly discovered that the dwelling units already planned would not be sufficient to meet the new demand. Consequently, an augmented and accelerated programme was implemented using, for the first time in Bermuda, modular housing on a large scale. With this provision, and funds for upgrading other sub-standard housing, some 1,500 units will be added but the shortfall will not be fully met immediately.

In addition to building houses between 1980–84, the Government undertook numerous other capital building projects among which were: Government Administration Building, a women's prison, a home for the handicapped, hospital extensions, school extensions, post offices, police accommodation, and a reverse osmosis water plant.

Shipwrecks

It was as a result of a shipwreck that Bermuda was developed in the way it has been but, even today, ships with modern navigational equipment still run aground on the offshore reefs. Lying as it does at the crossroads of four busy shipping lanes – from North America to South America, and from the Gulf of Mexico to Europe – many ships pass by without having a need to call. But, since 1972, twenty-four ships have run into difficulties in Bermuda's waters and several of them have run aground – thus posing serious pollution threats to the environment and ecology of the islands.

In 1979 the Liberian general cargo ship *Mari Boeing* landed on the Great Bermuda Reef ten miles off shore and remained there for three months. As a result of this incident the Bermuda Marine Pollution Contingency Plan Committee (MPCPC) was formally established in 1981 with a view to having coordinated inter-agency contingency mechanisms in place for dealing with such emergencies. That same year the

Eastern Mariner, in sinking condition, was given refuge off Bermuda. It was soon determined that her 10,000 tons of fertiliser, diamonium phosphate, was leaking into the sea, and her 500 tons of fuel oil also posed a serious threat to the marine environment of the shallow reefs. The vessel was ordered out to sea under the international Oil Pollution Convention 1971 and sank soon after clearing the channel. It was the first time such a sinking order had been used in the United Kingdom or colonies.

International attention was again on Bermuda's waters in March 1981 when the Israeli bulk carrier *Mezada* went down ninety miles southeast of Bermuda after her hatches stove-in in severe seas. Twenty-nine of thirty-one crew members lost their lives.

Thanks to an agreement Bermuda has with the United States Government, joint efforts of the US Coast Guard and Bermudians cleared the Liberian tanker *Tifoso* off the Bermuda Great Reef in 1983. After twelve days the ship was towed out to sea and sunk by explosives. The US Navy also is prepared to loan an oil barge and other facilities if they are needed.

1984 was a trying year at sea. In September and October, two large vessels were grounded within a period of fifteen days. First, the Maltese *Sealuck*, loaded with grain, ran aground on the Bermuda Great Reef west of North Rock. The salvage team removed 7,000 tons of grain and the US Navy barge removed 700 tons of her oil. Second, the Mexican tanker *Aguila Azteca*, containing 196,000 tons of heavy maya crude and 8,000 tons of bunkers, ran aground close to where the *Sealuck* had been refloated three days earlier. It took an international effort, involving the Dutch salvage company Smit-Tak International, to successfully refloat her ten days later – a time period when two hurricanes passed perilously close by.

After the 1983 *Tifoso* grounding the Bermuda Government requested the International Maritime Organization (IMO) in London, through the British Government, for a Prohibited Zone to be established north of Bermuda. However, the IMO did not grant the request so a further representation was made by Bermuda for the establishment of a 'Zone to be Avoided.' It was agreed upon subject to ratification by the full plenary session of the IMO in late 1985. The IMO regards Bermuda's MPCPC to be the best of its kind and has chosen Bermuda as the site for training senior personnel from the Caribbean for pollution control and planning.

Finally, in this sad account of sea tragedies, on 3 June 1984 the British registered tall ship, *Marques*, sank ninety miles to the north of Bermuda with a loss of nineteen lives. The *Marques* was taking part in the American Sail Training Association and British Sail Training Association Tall Ships' Race from Bermuda to Halifax, Nova Scotia. Only the day before she had left Bermuda in a fleet of thirty-nine sailing vessels, including four square riggers. The sixty-seven-year-old *Marques* was internationally known having played the three masted square rigger, HMS *Beagle* in the BBC's 'The Voyage of Charles Darwin'. Also, she had just won the San Juan to Bermuda leg of the Cutty Sark Tall Ships' Race.

On board was a crew of twenty-eight – mostly aged between fifteen and twenty-five and gathered for training from the UK, USA, Canada, and Antigua. After making good time at first she suffered a catastrophic knock down and sank within a minute. It was so sudden that there was no time for warnings and there were only nine survivors – picked up in modern life rafts by the Polish sailing vessel *Smuga Cienna* and the Canadian frigate HMCS *Assiniboine*. World-wide interest in this tragedy continues and a memorial fund has been established in the UK to raise funds for the families of those lost and to build a memorial replica of the *Marques*.

Bermuda's 375th Anniversary

Throughout 1984 Bermuda celebrated the 375th anniversary of the wreck of the *Sea Venture* and the beginning of human settlement on the islands. The official opening was performed by the Governor and the Mayor of St. George's on 2 January in King's Square, St. George's. During January, events such as exhibitions of arts, crafts, photographs, and boats were held but the highlight was a Period Ball featuring costumes dating from 1609 to the present. The other parishes carried out similar activities at suitable intervals throughout the year. Perhaps the climax of the celebrations was the four-day visit of HRH the Princess Margaret in October. She was welcomed by a 21-gun salute, a Bermuda Regiment guard of honour, and participated in many other events. She convened Parliament, opened the Bermuda Arts Centre, and unveiled a statue of Sir George Somers at Ordnance Island, St. George's, where a full-scale replica of the *Deliverance* also stands.

As a final historical glimpse, this tiny country has been poised on the threshold of independence for several years but, for now, Bermuda remains the oldest self-governing colony in the Commonwealth.

3 ASPECTS OF LIFE

Contemporary life in Bermuda is clearly linked with the country's physical environment and the historical determining factors which were dealt with earlier. In this chapter, some aspects of late twentieth century living are covered; particularly so far as the people, communications, and cultural customs are concerned. The major governmental interventions in day-to-day affairs of Bermudians are outlined in this, and in the next two chapters.

PEOPLE

Bermuda's human habitation began with the wrecking of the *Sea Venture* in 1609. In 1612, sixty settlers arrived in the *Plough* and ten years later Governor Butler estimated the population to be about 1,500. Just over 100 years later, in 1727, Governor John Hope gave the population as 8,270 – 4,470 white, 3,500 coloured. By 1833 the total number of people had risen to 9,195 of whom 4,297 were white, 3,612 were slaves, and 1,286 were free coloured. In 1940, the population was made up of 11,481 whites and 19,333 coloured – 30,814 in all. Forty years later, in 1980 (the most recent census), the total population (exclusive of foreign naval and military personnel) was 54,050 – 33,158 black and 20,892 white. Also, in that year, over 600,000 visitors landed on the shores. The Registrar General's latest published figures (end of 1983) show that the total population was 56,194 – officially broken down without mentioning colour or national origin into 27,420 males and 28,744 females.

The five major racial/ethnic groups found in Bermuda are: Bermudian whites, Bermudian blacks, Portuguese, West

Indians, and expatriates. As well, one percent of the population is made up of Chinese and East Indians. Racially then, blacks form approximately three-fifths of the resident population and slightly more than three-quarters of the native-born population.

The geographical and historical conditions described in the first two chapters brought about more than the usual amount of racial admixture. This is readily apparent in the Caucasian-like features of many Bermudian blacks. Yet, as Manning says the 'mulatto appearance has not been a source of social privilege [as prevails in the Caribbean] . . . All blacks, regardless of shading or social position, have traditionally been known simply as "coloured Bermudians". Middle-class standing in black society has been based on adoption of white values rather than inheritance of white appearance.' In his perceptive study, Manning identifies the Portuguese in Bermuda as serving the 'buffer function' provided by mulattoes in the West Indies. Comprising about one-tenth of the total population, the Portuguese have perpetuated their social enclave by largely retaining their native language and customs and by building their own recreational clubs. Most black and white Bermudians continue to regard the Portuguese as a separate, but well-accepted, group.

Manning describes the Bermudian-West Indian division as centering on 'what the two groups agreed were their defining attributes: a complacent and cavalier attitude toward life on the part of the Bermudians versus an aggressive and serious attitude on the part of West Indians.' The stereotypes persisted until after World War II but acculturation and intermarriage has been such that some third generations have been reached. However, the stereotype is easily recalled when West Indians have been recruited as policemen and their authority positions have brought them into conflict with black Bermudians. Successful West Indians are used as examples of how blacks can advance in the Bermudian civil service or professions. Alternatively, Manning cites people with leftist political views as often being accused of 'having West Indian blood in their veins' and hence being a cut below the 'coloured Bermudian' – either way the ethnic division is exacerbated.

The final significant group of people – the expatriates, are legally people residing on the island who do not possess Bermudian status. Colloquially, they are known as the foreign-born working force whose period of residence in Bermuda ranges from several months to intended permanency. They are politically and numerically significant for they constitute about 57 percent of Bermuda's white population, approximately 28 percent of the total population, and close to one-third of the labour force. Not counting the 29 percent foreign-born West Indians and Portuguese, more than half the expatriates are English and nearly a quarter are American; most of the remainder are Canadian or European. Manning describes the expatriates as 'authority figures and publicity agents of the colonial system.' That is, they are largely policemen, teachers, judges, civil servants, managers, doctors, nurses, and other professionals. Of course, many also fill more menial positions in the tourist industry as is seen in Chapter 5. Many expatriates, especially the English, form a 'floating population' – they do not stay long and often break employment contracts or leave after one three-year contract.

Overall, Manning sees the five major population groups forming 'more of a medley than a melting pot; they mix but do not combine . . . The central features of pluralism, in Bermuda . . . include the lack of common social will, the existence of culturally and institutionally separate groups in physical proximity, and the maintenance of controlling power in the hands of a minority who enforce the social order.'

In common with many parts of the Western world, the family in Bermuda appears to be losing some of its unity. Divorces have increased since 1970, children leave home earlier, fewer old people live out their lives in their own homes or with their children, and the sense of neighbourhood unity appears to have lessened in many parts of the island. Of course, many women work outside the home and, as Tucker notes, they 'have always undertaken a large share of public responsibilities.' It was the work of women in World War II which led to the passing of the Woman's Suffrage Bill in 1944. Incredibly, it now seems, before 1944 Bermuda's women were classed with children and lunatics so far as their voting rights were concerned. They had actively struggled for rights since 1898 – and particularly when England's women won enfranchisement in 1918.

WORKFORCE FEATURES

The population considerations together with the economic situation recorded in Chapter 5, present challenging problems to the Ministry of Labour and Home Affairs. In this section, particulars are given on how major workforce features are broadly accommodated with a view to achieving efficiency and harmony. Further occupational details are in Chapter 5.

Bermudian Status

Inherent in the policy on Bermudian Status is the Government's recognition that it is imperative for young Bermudians to be assured of having adequate career prospects; particularly in view of the improved educational opportunities which are currently available. Acquisition of Bermudian Status involves a quota under which status may be granted on a points system. The quota system is designed to relate proportionately to the total population of Bermudians, and is fixed at one-tenth of one percent of the population. At present, the maximum number of persons who may be granted status each year is forty. The points system was modified to its present form in 1978 with a view to providing equitable means for assessing candidates. It is divided into two sections – points awarded by the Ministry (maximum 75) and points awarded by the Status Committee (maximum 75).

The Ministry's points are based on factual information concerning the applicant such as his length of residence in Bermuda and his family associations in Bermuda. The Status Committee's assessment is discretionary but points are awarded based on the following considerations: (1) the economic situation of the islands and the due protection of persons already in gainful occupation; (2) the character and previous conduct of the applicant; (3) any advantage or disadvantage which the continued residence of the applicant or his family may afford to the islands; (4) the extent to which the applicant has become assimilated into the life and affairs of the islands; (5) the financial solvency and domestic ability of the applicant; and, (6) the desirability of giving preference to applicants married to persons already possessing Bermudian Status. Thus, the overriding aim is to ensure that Bermudian Status will continue to be granted to those persons whose skills and expertise are particularly needed, and who make valuable contributions to the economic and social development of the community. In recent years close to 200 people have applied for the status each year and close to forty people have been granted the status each year.

Residential Certificates

Residential Certificates may be granted under the Bermuda Immigration and Protection Act, 1956. They are granted at the Minister's discretion, but can be revoked without notice. The present policy is not to issue Residential Certificates unless applicants are retired persons of substantial financial means who are of good character and want to reside in Bermuda. Such people normally buy or rent high-priced properties and frequently invest money locally, employ domestics, and gardeners, etc. Therefore, they become an economic asset to Bermuda.

Residential Certificate holders are prohibited from engaging in gainful employment and must meet the following requirements: (a) must be a retired person with substantial means; or, (b) be the spouse of a person who possesses Bermudian Status; or (c) be a person who was employed in Bermuda for at least six months and now wishes to retire in Bermuda; or (d) be a person who owns property in Bermuda. In recent years the following number of non-Bermudians have been granted Residential Certificates: 48 (1979), 46 (1980), 29 (1981), 13 (1982), 56 (1983).

Deportees

It is sometimes necessary to deport foreign nationals from Bermuda – usually people who have been convicted of a criminal offence and who have served a prison term. The numbers are: 25 (1979), 18 (1980), 20 (1981), 5 (1982), 6

(1983). As well, some foreign nationals are asked to leave by the Minister while others are placed on the Stop List – in 1983, eighty-three were stop-listed of whom forty-three were undesirables and forty other cases involved drugs.

Portuguese Accord

Ever since 1848 there has been a steady flow of Portuguese nationals, mostly from the Azores, into Bermuda which has formed an important part of the workforce. Over the years various agreements have been signed between the two governments covering the workers' terms of employment. The latest agreement, an accord between the Government of Bermuda and the Government of the Republic of Portugal, was signed in December 1982. The accord covers the general terms and conditions of employment and residence of Portuguese contract workers. Generally it brings the Portuguese workers into line with the employment of other nationals and they are no longer restricted to the job categories of farm workers, dairymen, gardeners, and kitchen helpers. At the end of 1983, there were 956 Portuguese workers covered under the 1982 Accord and thirty-one approved applications were pending for workers to enter Bermuda as gardeners, farm workers, and hotel kitchen helpers.

Employment Generally

Bermuda's employment policy is to achieve Bermudianisation where possible, without lowering the standards of efficiency or service. Qualified Bermudians must have, and in law do have, first claim to any job. Though the Government thinks Bermudians should rightfully aspire to any job, it also believes that Bermudian birth is not, in itself, sufficient qualification if Bermuda is to prosper. However, the immigration policy is designed to reduce, in a systematic and orderly way, the number of employed non-Bermudians. Thus, certain job categories have been closed to non-Bermudians and employers are being encouraged to make greater efforts to employ Bermudians. Nevertheless, there are presently more jobs than Bermudians available to fill them and so overseas recruitment must continue for the time being.

Trade Unions

Trade Unions came late to Bermuda even though there had been many historical instances of industrial unrest. Of the unions currently existing, the first was the Bermuda Union of Teachers which was organised in 1919. It is now called the Amalgamated Bermuda Union of Teachers, having joined forces with the Teachers' Association of Bermuda, and has 700 members. Over the years it has done much to improve schools and obtain better conditions for teachers. Industrial trade unionism appeared in Bermuda much later, in fact, when the Americans were building the base during World War II. Wage disparities between those wages received by local workers during the hard economic times and those paid by the Americans led to the formation of the Bermuda Workers' Association, a forerunner of the Bermuda Industrial Union which now has 6,000 members.

Other unions, with their approximate membership numbers in brackets are: Bermuda Public Services Association (1,450), Bermuda Federation of Musicians (310), Electricity Supply Trade Union (180), Bermuda Cable and Wireless Association (55), Fire Association (45), Bermuda Employers' Council (300), Hotel Employers (28), and the Association of School Principals (35). This gives a total trade union membership of 9,111. As well, though not legally trade unions, the Police Association and the Prison Officers' Association (400 members in all) are recognised by the Government for the purpose of collective bargaining. Broadly, the Government's Department of Labour's objectives are to promote good industrial relations through advisory conciliation and arbitration in the prevention and settlement of industrial disputes. And, to ensure compliance with international labour standards as laid down by the International Labour Office Conventions and Recommendations applicable to Bermuda.

LAND AND HOUSING

In this segment the land use structure of Bermuda is described before tracing the history of housing and explaining the Government's present housing policies.

Land Use Structure

The source of this information is the Bermuda Development Plan 1983 which was kindly made available by the Department of Planning. To explain the following land use structure table, this introduction provides a guide to the meaning of the various density classifications and zonings: (1) High Density – intensive residential development with a broad range of commercial services; (2) Medium Density – low to medium residential with a limited range of commercial services; (3) Clustered Low Density – clustered housing to preserve open space; (4) Garden District – low density residential with an emphasis on vegetation; (5) Rural – intended to preserve large parcels of land and countryside; (6) Major Hotel/Cottage Colony – to accommodate major tourist accommodation and provide for any expansion of tourism; (7) Major Industrial – designated employment centres specifically for industrial and warehouse development; (8) Special Government – to provide for a range of uses and building types to meet the special needs of government; and, (9) Open Space Area – for the preservation of Bermuda's limited supply of open land so as to retain a balance between developed and undeveloped land.

The economic significance of the land use data is dealt with in Chapter 5 while more particulars of the towns and settlements are included in Chapter 6.

Housing History

Traditionally, the provision of housing in Bermuda has been by the private sector, except that in Colonial times the Royal Navy and the British Army provided housing for married servicemen and for civilian staff. After World War II, when the British services' presence ended, the housing stock was conveyed to the Bermuda Government which has now vested it in the Housing Corporation and in the West End Development Corporation, a statutory corporation which has been set up to redevelop the old Royal Navy lands. This west end British housing constituted the major part of the available rental housing.

Private development generally comprised one building, containing two apartments, on a single lot. One dwelling was

Lush vegetation surrounding an old style private home. Note the 'welcoming arm steps' and a present-day horse drawn carriage

occupied by the owner whose tenant lived in the other; and the rent helped the owner meet his mortgage commitments. Mortgages were non-amortised and the interest, which accumulated at a statutory rate of 7 percent per annum, was usually paid quarterly.

When the Housing Corporation was established in 1973, and started providing mortgage funds for new construction by first-time home owners, it applied maximum size criteria related to the numbers of bedrooms in a unit and this has served to reduce the overall size of apartments. The Corporation will lend up to 85 percent (formerly, traditionally 60 percent) of the estimated value of the completed project and its mortgage servicing criteria are less stringent than those of traditional lenders. Interestingly, though the Corporation's clients are usually people who have been turned down by commercial lenders, there have been no forced sales and the arrears situation is negligible.

Thus, the agency charged with the responsibility of ensuring that Bermudians have adequate affordable shelter has made impressive contributions. Prior to 1973 the Government had constructed 179 units; at the end of 1985 the Government's total contribution to the housing stock was 1,654 units, or about 8 percent of all of Bermuda's housing stock, at a total cost of $110.25 million. The innovative Danish modular, or prefabricated, structures have certainly helped the programme. They are built from pre-cast, light weight,

(*opposite, top left*) *Deliverance* replica. Visitors to St. George's. Bermuda's capital until 1815, stop near a nineteenth century cannon for a chat with the town crier. In the background lies a replica of the *Deliverance*, one of two ships built in 1610 to carry stranded passengers to Virginia after the wrecking of the *Sea Venture*

(*top right*) Ducking Stool. 'Let this be a warning,' shouts the St. George's town crier to tourists witnessing the seventeenth century punishment for wives who nagged their husbands

(*below*) Enchanting harbour. The south side of Hamilton's harbour presents a picturesque scene as a ferryboat approaches the Salt Kettle terminal in Paget

1981 Land Use Structure by Parish (Acres)*

Parish	High Density	Medium Density	Clust'd Low Density	Garden District	Rural	Major Hotel/ Cottage Colony	Major Industrial	Special Gov't	Open Space	Total
Sandys	242	112	34	152	203	34	7	50	358	1,192
Southampton	114	385	9	200	26	25	12	4	606	1,381
Warwick	340	176	27	119	44	40	3	7	599	1,355
Paget	47	267	20	369	67	90	–	8	380	1,248
Pembroke	501	3	25	280	–	17	78	–	361	1,265
Devonshire	333	124	2	123	52	9	4	43	473	1,163
Smith's	52	354	15	217	70	19	–	–	413	1,140
Hamilton	154	118	36	189	33	25	11	31	592	1,189
St. George's	246	45	16	223	13	30	34	50	710	1,367
Total	2,029	1,584	184	1,872	508	289	149	193	4,492	11,300

*2.471 acres equals 1 hectare

reinforced concrete panels which can be produced with finished interior and exterior surfaces, thus having great design flexibility since virtually any panel size can be produced. Interestingly, also the Government's injection of $20 million over the last two years into the mortgage market has made a major impact on the economy of the construction industry. Virtually all the money has been spent with small contractors and thus helped them to prosper.

Policies and Planning

It is still current Government policy, through the Housing Corporation mortgage programme, to increase the number of Bermudians who own their own homes. Expediently, the Corporation has also acted as a developer in recent years but, as soon as economic factors permit, it is intended that the private sector will be left with the developers' role. As well as encouraging and assisting the private sector to develop for Bermudian ownership, the Corporation will begin a scheme designed to sell existing rental units to sitting tenants. Amortised mortgages of up to 100 percent will be made available to tenants who are deemed to be financially able to meet the mortgage payments.

So far as non-Bermudians are concerned a land acquisition policy has been in effect since 1979. Currently it, (a) prohibits the sale of undeveloped land to non-Bermudians; (b) permits local and locally operated exempt companies to lease any new residential house with an Annual Rental Value (ARV) of at least $24,000 (other than condominiums) for a period of up to twenty-one years; and, (c) prohibits the sale of houses to non-Bermudians unless the ARV is $37,000 or over. Also, non-Bermudians are prohibited from obtaining a licence to acquire an apartment or condominium unless it has an ARV of not less than $13,200 and that the buyer, (a) has a Residential Certificate; (b) is the spouse of a person who possesses Bermudian Status and wishes to own an apartment or condominium jointly with his or her Bermudian spouse; or, (c) is the son, daughter, mother, or father of the owner of an apartment or condominium and will take that dwelling by voluntary conveyance or under a will subject, however, to the exercise by the Minister of Home Affairs of discretion in special cases.

Overall, these policies seem to be achieving their aims because, in 1979, 9.09 ha (22.481 acres) were sold to Bermudians by non-Bermudians; in 1980 it was 5.86 ha (14.4948 acres) and 9.30 ha (22.995 acres) in 1981. In 1982, 2.39 ha (5.927 acres) were sold to non-Bermudians by Bermudians; in 1983, 2.67 ha (6.620 acres) were sold to non-Bermudians by Bermudians while 3.36 ha (8.308 acres) were acquired by Bermudians from non-Bermudians.

Clearly, the finite small size of Bermuda, and the very short supply of developable land, make it essential that any development that does occur meets the requirements of the Development Plan 1983 in 'maintaining and enhancing the environmental character of Bermuda and the Bermuda image.' There is no definition of 'The Bermuda image' – it is in the eye of the beholder but it does not include high rise development (no residential developments currently exceed three storeys). However, five storey blocks of apartments, set into a hillside, with third floor access are on the drawing board. It is likely that this form of development will be the pattern for the future; but, redevelopment will be a slow and painstaking process as individual lots have to be consolidated into large enough tracts to make the new building viable.

Certainly the authorities in Bermuda have made great progress towards achieving their land and housing objectives. The Department of Planning's overall function is to prepare and implement planning policy for all of Bermuda. Its three basic responsibilities are: the planning and control of orderly development; the protection of the environment; and, the maintenance of proper building construction standards. Now part of a reorganised Ministry of the Environment, it has programmes in place to continue its fine progress.

COMMUNITY, CULTURE, AND RELIGION

The Community in General

In general, and relatively to other modern Western societies, the Bermuda people form a closely-knit community. Everyone seems to know everyone else – either by family ties, friendships, neighbourhoods, school and business associations, cultural groups, or recreational organisations. Until recently, mail deliverers could and would deliver mail merely by the addressee's name and parish. Similarly, taxi drivers found no problems with directions like, 'Smith's pink house at the top of the hill in Warwick.'

Community Services

Overall, the Ministry of Community and Cultural Affairs is responsible for many related programmes. Its Department of Community Services coordinates major activities including heritage celebrations, and recreation for senior citizens, disabled people, and community groups. The Consumer Affairs Bureau provides consumer information and advice to the public by way of sponsored talks, workshops, posters, pamphlets, slide presentations, and newspaper articles. As well, it regularly deals with consumer complaints.

The Community Education and Development Project is operated through two community evening schools and extends the usual educational role to one which identifies needs, wants, and community problems. It then assists in developing facilities, programmes, staff, and leadership to help enhance the entire community. About 800 residents annually pay small fees for courses in such activities as computer operations, business studies, home improvement, photography, the arts, sports, and fitness. The programme is designed to help people of varying ages, cultural heritages, religious beliefs, and socio-economic backgrounds to learn to play, study, and work together on an equal basis.

Small Business Development Corporation

The Small Business Development Corporation assists small businesses with technical and financial help in the form of guaranteeing loans of up to $50,000. Generally, the businesses it assists are independently owned and operated, not dominant in their particular field and they operate for the purpose of business profit.

Human Rights Commission

The Human Rights Commission began its work, in May 1982, to monitor and improve race relations; it is regarded as an important step on the road to social justice for all Bermudians. The Act sets out to reaffirm the rights and freedom enshrined in Bermuda's Constitution and to protect Bermudians, and other bona fide residents of the islands, against most forms of discrimination. It prohibits discrimination on the grounds of race, colour, ancestry, place of origin, sex, marital or family status, being born out of wedlock, religious or political beliefs in the areas of employment, business transactions, leisure activities, public services, and accommodation.

The twelve-member Commission's primary function is to investigate complaints of unlawful discrimination and to provide redress if the complaints are substantiated. As well, the Commission acts in an educational and advisory capacity by informing people of their rights and obligations under the Act.

Holidays

There are ten official public holidays each year: New Year's Day, Good Friday, Bermuda Day, Queen's Birthday, Cup Match, Somers' Day, Labour Day, Remembrance Day, Christmas Day, and Boxing Day. Three of these days have particular community appeal: Good Friday, Bermuda Day, and Cup Match (described later in this chapter). There is a kite-flying tradition on Good Friday which probably brings out the largest number of kite enthusiasts per capita in the western world. Thousands of kites of all shapes, sizes, and colours fill the sky in a confetti-like pattern. Most children fly a kite as part of a tradition which reaches into Bermudian folklore. Apparently a Sunday school teacher wanted to illustrate the New Testament story of Christ's ascension so he built a simple cross-stick kite with the image of Christ painted on its surface. With children attentive he launched the kite from a hill and when it reached maximum height he cut the string so that the kite became a speck to the children before it disappeared!

Bermuda Day is 24 May when Bermuda's cultural heritage

is brought into focus. It now celebrates the transition of whites, blacks, and Portuguese becoming integrated during the 1960s. The integration was accomplished with a minimum of discord so that today blacks and whites are learning to live and grow together. And to appreciate the differences as well as the similarities in each other's heritage. The day is celebrated with school performances, ethnic events, a half marathon, and a festive parade of floral floats, marching bands, majorettes, and carnival dancers.

The Bermuda Library

Sir William Reid, one of Bermuda's best governors, founded the Bermuda Library in 1839. Today the Main Library, two branches, and a Youth Library hold 150,000 volumes and, in addition, the Library has subscriptions to over 100 periodicals and newspapers. The reference section of the Main Library contains an extensive Bermudian collection of books, newspapers, pamphlets, maps, and other items of local interest. Much of the material is catalogued in a National Bibliography. Further, a comprehensive collection of Bermuda's colonial records is preserved in the Bermuda Archives which also operates the Government's Central Micrographic Unit.

Bermuda Arts Council

Established in 1969, the Bermuda Arts Council Act makes provision for the Council to function with a minimum of five members and a maximum of eleven – all of whom are appointed annually by the Governor. The Council's aims are: (1) to develop and improve the knowledge, understanding, and practice of the arts; (2) to increase the accessibility of the arts whether by means of festivals of the arts, or otherwise, to the public, throughout Bermuda; and (3) to advise and cooperate with government departments, art groups, art societies, and other bodies on any matter concerned with the foregoing points.

By means of its restricted government grant the Council, in turn, has made funds available to arts groups and has initiated its own programmes which have included summer festivals, sponsorship of performing groups, educational drama, and loans, scholarships, or grants for students of visual, fine, and performing arts. It is hoped that, eventually, Bermudians' latent talents will be developed as opportunities for creative expression are enhanced. To date, according to W. S. Zuill, the Bermuda people have only developed two forms of art – architecture and Gombey dancing. An example of the former may be seen in the restored State House which has the Italian style decorative entrance, thick walls for coolness and to withstand hurricanes, and a flat roof. Dating back to the mid-eighteenth century the Gombey dances are an amalgamation of influences from Africa, Britain, the West Indies, and the American Indians. Costumes are colourful and most Bermudians flock to see the performances in the Christmas season and in May when they hear the drum, the whistle, and the pounding feet.

The Bermuda National Trust

Based on the work of the Bermuda Historical Monuments Trust, which was founded in 1937, the Bermuda National Trust started in 1970 as a conservation trust based on the constitution of the National Trust of England, Wales, and Northern Ireland though suitably adapted for island needs. Its motto is, 'For places of Historic Interest or Natural Beauty' and its aims are carried out through ownership of land and buildings, and through lobbying for careful development throughout the islands. Most notable of the Trust's buildings are its three museums: Verdmont (Smith's Parish), Tucker House (St. George's), and the Confederate Museum in the Globe Hotel at St. George's. Among the reserves the Trust owns are Spittal Pond bird sanctuary and Paget Marsh (endemic and native flora). As well as owning a number of smaller reserves, all of which are open to the public, the Trust has recently formed an alliance with the Walsingham Trust, which owns Bermuda's first formally constituted nature reserve. Also, the Trust cooperates with organisations such as the Audubon Society, and publishes related scholarly works.

Religion

There are more than 100 churches dotted all over the islands which represent many faiths. Anglicans were among the original settlers 375 years ago and now there is at least one Anglican church in each parish. St. Peter's, constructed in 1612, is the oldest Anglican church in continuous use in the western hemisphere. There were some parochial and international squabbles in the historically dominant Church of England. Originally, Bermuda was under the jurisdiction of the diocese of London, then transferred to the see of Nova Scotia, and from 1839 to 1925 formed part of the diocese of Newfoundland. However, for more than fifty years now Bermuda has had its own bishop.

There are six Roman Catholic churches with the first being established in 1858. One bishop and seven priests serve the approximately 7,500 members. The numbers of Roman Catholics more than doubled between 1950 and 1970 – Portuguese immigration being a significant factor.

About 700 people attend the Presbyterian Church of Scotland which also has its roots in early Bermuda history (1719). The Salvation Army started in Bermuda eighty-eight years ago and now has eight churches and about 1,000 members. As well, it provides valuable services to help people in need. The Seventh Day Adventist Church began in 1901 and now has eight churches and 2,300 members – it is perhaps the fastest growing church on the islands and has attracted many younger people. The Wesleyan Methodist Church dates back to the 1600s and now has ten churches while other denominations are: Brethren, Baptists, Christian Science, Church of Nazarene, Church of Christ, Evangelical, Jehovah's Witnesses, Lutheran, Apostolic, Church of God, Pentecostal, Church of God of Prophecy, Shiloh, United Holy Churches, the Church of Jesus Christ of Latter Day Saints, and Unity. As well, Muslims have practised since 1960 and now have 300 members while the Ethiopian Orthodox Church, which was introduced in 1975, has about 400 members. There are no synagogues or rabbis in Bermuda but the Jewish community meets on the first Friday of every month and on major religious days at the chapel of the US Naval Base, and/or in private homes.

Clearly, there is religious freedom in Bermuda and,

according to Government data, most families are affiliated with a church and about 40 percent of people attend church regularly.

SPORTS AND RECREATION

The physical environment gives Bermuda ideal conditions for sports and virtually every well known sport is played in some form or another. Indeed sports are an integral part of life in Bermuda, often dominating the social calendar and providing leisure-time pursuits for a considerable proportion of the population. If current major sports have to be identified, it is safe to say that soccer dominates the winter scene while cricket is the national summertime sporting obsession.

Cricket

Cup Match is Bermuda's premier cricket event and the islands' version of midsummer madness. A carnival atmosphere prevails as people don their most outlandish fashions and head for the cricket field, where they enjoy the game, socialise, and sample food from the many stalls that ring the outfield. Although cricket is popular throughout the Commonwealth, only Bermuda grinds to a complete halt for two days every summer and turns its attention to a game of cricket. Cup Match takes place on the Thursday and Friday before the first Monday in August and pits the best of Somerset Cricket Club, located at the islands' west end, against their counterparts of the St. George's Cricket Club, from the east end. The fans are always there early with their shade umbrellas and picnic hampers containing ample supplies of food and drink. Also, Cup Match is one of the few occasions when gambling is openly permitted in Bermuda. Although thousands flock to the cricket match, thousands of others head to the beaches, camp sites, and picnic grounds – but always with a radio on hand to listen to the Cup Match scores.

Cricket was first played in Bermuda in the 1840s by officers and men of the British garrison and Americans and Australians played in Hamilton's Cricket Week during the 1890s.

Cup Match originated in 1902, when a group of Bermudians organised a friendly cricket game between two fraternal lodges. The lodge games became so popular that workers would absent themselves from work as 'sick' on cricket days. Frustrated employers had no choice but to press to make the holiday official and that was finally done in 1947 – making it Bermuda's most popular holiday ever since.

The cricket season runs from late April through late September when league games are played on weekends. A special under-19 programme was established ten years ago and it has greatly increased participation in the sport and produced a few budding Cup Match future stars. Also, Bermudians have been exposed to international standard cricket with overseas players taking part in special tournaments in Bermuda, and also by travelling abroad to compete with teams in other countries.

Soccer

Though without a cup match comparable to cricket's, soccer is nevertheless an extremely popular sport which begins each September and ends the following April when the two top teams of the first division of the league play-off for the Bermuda Football Association Cup. Throughout the season, usually on Sunday afternoons and some week nights, players enjoy their play in first, second, or commercial league games. Interest and competition is keen amongst players and fans alike, providing a main topic of conversation for young and old. Fans are fiercely loyal to their teams and turn out in droves to support them.

The junior programme has attracted hundreds of young players and each first division club has a youth team. Island-wide competition takes place on Saturday mornings throughout the season and, from the best players, a National Youth Squad is selected.

Bermuda has yet to reach the final round of Olympic competition but it does play internationally and has competed in the Pan American Games.

Tennis

Tucker recounts how Thomas Middleton saw tennis played in England in 1873 and then brought a 'set' of equipment to Bermuda. On arrival he thought tennis might be 'a shade inelegant and unrefined for ladies' so he gave the equipment to the Gray family in Paget where Sir Brownlow Gray promptly laid out Bermuda's first court. Soon others were playing and Bermuda's first tennis tournament was held in the grounds of Admiralty House, Pembroke, in 1877. Meanwhile, in 1874, Mary Outerbridge took equipment and a rule book to New York and obtained permission to mark out the United States' first court at the Staten Island Cricket Club.

Tennis is very popular in Bermuda where about 100 courts are available for public use at hotels, guest houses, or at two Government-owned locations – the Government Tennis Stadium and the Port Royal Tennis Courts, adjacent to the golf course. Many courts are floodlit for night play and tournaments are held throughout the year.

Golf

The very sight of Bermuda's golf courses is enough to make anyone realise that it is an ideal location for the game. The islands have eight golf courses which offer spectacular ocean views, undulating fairways, and truly immaculate conditions. The most challenging courses are the 18-hole par 71 Mid Ocean Golf Club course, which is private, and the Government owned Port Royal Golf Course. Both were designed by Robert Trent-Jones and are considered to be among the world's finest. He also designed Bermuda's recently constructed course at the new St. George's Club and Club Med, which will serve club players and the general public. The most popular annual contest is the Goodwill Golf Tournament which is held in December, while most other tournaments take place between November and April even though golf is played throughout the year.

Running

The 1970s running craze did not miss Bermuda which now hosts some excellent international events on tough courses.

The most notable are the International 10K and the International Marathon, which are run during the last weekend in January. The races attract top international runners as well as many other keen participants – the 1983 and 1984 races had more than 800 competitors in the 10K and 400 in the marathon.

Then, of course, Bermudians have their own 13-mile race on 24 May which is only open to locals. In recent years the course has been from Somerset to the National Stadium in Devonshire. It's a gruelling race, usually run in heat and humidity, but it nevertheless attracts about 400 runners.

Water Sports

Water sports, from deep-sea diving, to scuba diving, to snorkelling and fishing are understandably popular in Bermuda where the waters are the clearest in the Atlantic and colourful sights abound on the reefs. Sailing races, organised by the Royal Bermuda Yacht Club, are held every Saturday from January to November while the Bermuda Offshore Cruising Association holds races on the first Sunday of each month. The spectacular Bermuda fitted dinghies race on alternate Sundays during spring, summer, and autumn, beginning on 24 May.

Of course, Bermuda is internationally famous in the sailing community for the Bermuda Rig, the lofty, triangular fore-and-aft mainsail of modern racing and cruising yachts. Its prototype is generally held to be the 'shoulder-of-mutton' rig used on ships' boats and other small naval vessels, and it was first seen in about 1808 in the Bermudas. In its original form it consisted of a tall mast, raking well aft, and a loose-footed sail with a sprit to hold it out instead of a boom. As developed for use in yachts the mast was lengthened considerably, being well stayed with spreaders for strength, and the foot of the sail was shortened. This was to give the long 'leading edge' to the sail, the ratio of height (or hoist) to foot being as high as 2.5 to 1 on small yachts, although 2 to 1 or 1.5 to 1 is more common in yachts over fifty feet long. In its modified form the rig did not come into general use in yachts outside Bermuda until after 1918, but between World Wars I and II its advantages in efficiency and ease of handling became widely appreciated so that by the 1950s, it had been adopted throughout the world in most auxiliary yachts as well as in racing yachts and dinghies.

Also on the water, windsurfing regattas, organised by the Bermuda Boardsailing Association, are held every Sunday from April through December. For those who would rather watch boat racing from the safety of land there are power-boat races on Sundays from May through December at Ferry Reach, a calm strip of water near the Bermuda airport.

In the water, organised swimming increased dramatically in the 1970s with the construction of two new half-Olympic-size pools and the formation of local clubs. Also, schools offer swimming as part of the physical education programme. Clubs now have regular competitions and compete with a number of overseas teams.

Other Recreational Provisions

Sports and recreation for old and young are coordinated by the Govenment's Department of Youth, Sport, and Recreation, which maintains and operates 29.94 ha (74 acres) of property. It includes the National Stadium, Tennis Stadium, and the Softball Stadium. Camp sites, such as Port's Island, White's Island, Darrell's Island, and Messina House, are part of the acreage. Camps are used by 23,000 people annually, but their use in summer is restricted to local groups. The Department also operates St. George's and Pembroke Youth Centres which provide social and cultural programmes daily after school for eighty youngsters. The Government additionally makes annual grants to youth organisations such as Sea Cadets, Girl Guides, Boy Scouts, and to sports governing bodies.

Beyond the scope of this book, but nevertheless fascinating, is the whole play world found in the black clubs of Bermuda. The clubs began as an obvious reaction to earlier segregation but Manning estimated that the fourteen clubs have about 5,000 members, and some members are now white. Manning's book is a scrupulously documented study which is filled with lively, humorous, and perceptive insights into the role of black clubs in modern Bermudian culture and political life. All of the book is well worth reading but his final theory is most perceptive for he says, 'In Bermuda the play and prosperity made possible by tourism do not function to denigrate the native tradition in favour of foreign substitutes. Nor do they inhibit progressive movements or sustain a racial inferiority complex. On the contrary, club play symbolizes a set of meanings that rejuvenate the indigenous cultural tradition and that promote the process of social change by making it comprehensible and appealing to the people.' If this theory holds it is most likely goods news for Bermuda.

TRANSPORT

All transportation issues are largely the responsibility of the Bermuda Government and are administered through the Ministry of Transport Services. The Minister's road transport policies, which are the business of the Public Service Vehicles Licensing Board and of various advisory committees, are carried out through the Director of the Transport Control Department. It licenses garages, automobile mechanics, cycle liveries, vehicles, and drivers – as well as examining the latter.

Automobiles

After a bitter debate in the 1946 Bermuda Legislature it became possible for an individual to own a car or motorcycle for private use. The thought at the time among the lawmakers was that the cost of vehicles and the licence fees would prevent all but a few from owning cars. Alas, that was not so.

Now Bermuda has restrictions on the ownership of private cars and only residents are allowed to drive cars; there are no rental cars. Further, Bermuda does not recognise any other driving licence so that new residents must pass the Bermuda test before being allowed to drive. Visitors wishing to transport themselves normally hire mopeds or auxiliary cycles.

Also, to limit car ownership, the Government has been forced to adopt stringent control measures. Each residential unit may only have one car which may only be driven by members of that household, or by any licensed driver if a member of the household is in the car. Presently, 43,359 vehicles are registered; these include private cars, public service vehicles, trucks, mopeds, and other motor-assisted cycles. Clearly this is enough in an area of about 53.35 sq km (21 square miles) and only 200 km (125 miles) of public roads – so much so that discussions are taking place on the possibilities of further restrictions.

Apart from the regulations mentioned thus far there are others governing car sizes, engine sizes, commercial vehicle use restrictions, vehicle testing, bodywork testing, transfer of ownership, and the demolition of cars. The legal age for driving an auxiliary cycle is sixteen years; eighteen years for cars, motor cycles, and scooters. Visitors do not require a licence to drive auxiliary cycles but must be at least sixteen years old. Road rules include 'keep left,' pass on the right, maximum speed 35 kph (25 kph in St. George's), and safety helmets must be worn by all persons riding motorised cycles.

Taxis

Though the Government controls fares, dress standards of taxi drivers, and restricts the total number of taxis to 562 all vehicles are privately owned. Some drivers are also certified as tour guides and are excellent.

Buses

The Bermuda Public Transportation Board operates a fleet of

(*opposite*) Fort St. Catherine. Located at the easternmost tip of the islands in St. George's, the ramparts overlook the emerald waters of Sea Venture Flat where the first settlers were shipwrecked. The thick-walled fort was part of an early defence system built in 1612 by Bermuda's first governor, Richard Moore

Fort Scaur. In contrast this nineteenth century fortress was built to protect the RN Dockyard on Ireland Island. It is now a picnic ground with magnificent views over Ely's Harbour and the Great Sound

(*overleaf*) Gombey dances date back to the mid-eighteenth century and are an amalgamation of influences from Africa, Britain, the West Indies, and the American Indians

101 diesel-powered buses over eleven different routes which cover the main islands in all directions. As well as providing regularly scheduled services, the Board runs a school service, charters, and sightseeing buses to meet the requirements of commuters, shoppers, students, and visitors. In 1983, twenty new Belgian model buses with automatic transmission, wrap-around windows, good seats, and better ventilation were added to the system and have proven to be popular with both passengers and operators. Services begin daily at 6:15am and continue until 12:45am the following morning, making 500 trips per day in the peak season (April to October) carrying about 15,000 people. Since 1977, an exact fare system has been in place with discounts offered on booklets containing fifteen tickets and special cheaper fares for disabled people and senior citizen residents. Bus tokens form part of the fare structure for use by adults on the 3 and 14 zone rides.

Ferries

Visitors to Bermuda find the ferry service an ideal way to travel into the City of Hamilton from Somerset, Warwick, and Paget. The Government's Department of Marine and Ports Services operates the vessels which originate in Hamilton Harbour before crossing the Great Sound to Somerset Island. Boats, which carried 406,138 passengers in 1982, run from 7:15am until 11:55pm with the fare being $1.00 each way on the Warwick/Paget route. For a ride to any of the four docks in Sandys Parish the fare is $2.00 each way.

Shipping

The Minister of Transport is also responsible, through the Department of Marine and Ports, for the general manage-

(*opposite*) A wee bit of Scotland in Bermuda. Many Bermudians have Scottish ancestors. Every Wednesday at noon, December through March, this band of pipers and drummers gather at Fort Hamilton to perform as part of the Rendezvous programme. The group also participates in the Beat the Retreat Ceremony

Beat the Retreat is a ceremonial duty of the Bermuda Regiment performed in various locations around the island from April through October

ment, control, and supervision of all maritime matters. The Director of Marine and Ports Services is advised by a corporate body – The Ports Authority – consisting of between nine and eleven members appointed by the Minister.

The Department exercises general supervision and control over the navigation and berthing of ships and boats in Bermuda's territorial waters. Two pilot cutters, the *St. George* and the *St. David*, manned by shift crews working out of Market Wharf, Ordnance Island, St. George's, meet commercial vessels entering and leaving Bermuda. The pilot station at Fort George is manned on a shift basis by eleven branch pilots and a pilot warden who are available for duty 365 days a year. A training wall has been built on the south side of Town Cut Channel to improve passage and make it safer for ships entering and leaving Town Cut Channel.

Hamilton, the main place for shipping traffic, offers modern port facilities which can accommodate vessels up to 7.92 m (26 ft) in draught and has 232 sq m (2,500 sq ft) of berthing space together with some 4,275 sq m (46,000 sq ft) of shed space. A five-and-one-half acre container park with 198.1 m (650 ft) of quay was completed in 1973. Three cruise ships and two cargo ships have been accommodated at the same time on occasions. Hamilton is a port of British Registry, where vessels have been registered since the late 1790s. Ships registered in Bermuda are British registered ships and fly the British Red Ensign. In 1984, there was a total of 211 ships registered with a gross tonnage of 746,328 tonnes. The laws governing registration, ownership, transfer, and so on are contained in the Merchant Shipping Act 1984 which may be obtained from the Registry of Shipping, P.O. Box HM1628, Hamilton 5.

Cruise ships and a small amount of cargo are also handled in St. George's, which has modern port facilities. Cruise ships of up to 182 m (600 ft) in length and 7.92 m (26 ft) draught berth at Ordnance Island while Penno's Wharf provides facilities for vessels up to 8.53 m (28 ft) draught and has 1,394 sq m (15,000 sq ft) of shed space. On the north side of St. George's Island is an oil terminal for the reception of oil products and for bunkers, owned and operated by Esso

Bermuda. The dockyard at Ireland Island has the 243.82 m (800 ft) Commercial Wharf in the South Basin which has a depth of 10.05 m (33 ft). There are reception facilities for bulk cement and a bunkering station operated by the Shell Company of Bermuda.

Bermuda Harbour Radio's function is to serve as a rescue coordination centre and communications centre for search and rescue operations in the area. It keeps a constant watch on international maritime distress frequencies of 500 kHz, 2,182, and Channel 16 VHF. The station is also in direct contact with the US Coast Guard in New York and other rescue coordination centres in the US and in the Caribbean. The radar station at Fort George Hill, St. George's overlooks the main shipping channels and their approaches so as to provide surveillance of two-thirds of Bermuda's offshore waters and reefline. With an increasing number of yachts visiting Bermuda – 1,117 in 1984 – radar plays a vital part in helping to ensure their safe approach to the islands.

Civil Aviation

The Ministry of Transport's Department of Civil Aviation is responsible for carrying out civil aviation policy under Bermuda laws. Also, the Director of Civil Aviation is responsible for applying the United Kingdom Air Navigation (Overseas Territories) Order 1977 as it applies to Bermuda.

The airfield and technical services are provided by the US Navy in accordance with a treaty agreement between the Governments of the United States and the United Kingdom. Within the base is the Bermuda Air Terminal, which is operated by the Bermuda Government and handles all civil traffic. Bermuda is served by the following airlines with scheduled direct services from: Canada – Air Canada; Caribbean – British Airways; U.K. – British Airways; USA – American Airlines, Delta Airlines, Eastern Airlines, and Pan American. Since 1983, Bermuda has had a new charter flight policy to maintain some degree of control of such flights into and out of the islands. Flights to the United States from Bermuda are normally pre-cleared in Bermuda through US

Government facilities as far as customs, immigration, and health formalities are concerned.

There are no internal flights in Bermuda but the terminal is a busy one, handling 4,311 commercial aircraft arrivals in 1983 as well as 653 private aircraft arrivals. At the end of 1983, there were forty-four aircraft on the Bermuda Registry of which three were locally based/privately owned and operated solely in local airspace.

COMMUNICATIONS

Postal Services

Joseph Stockdale started postal services in Bermuda just over 200 years ago in 1784, when letters were carried on horseback with the letter carrier blowing a horn to alert residents of his approach. By 1787, Stockdale's service was only provided once a week and that arrangement lasted until 1812 when a government-operated postal service was established. Various attempts to establish international mail services were made in the 1780s but it was not until 1807 that a regular monthly service for overseas mail was established; it was instigated by the British when they built a naval dockyard for the British Fleet at the western end of the islands.

Today the Post Office Department handles 50 million pieces of mail each year and is one of the islands' most vital communication links with the international community. There is the General Post Office in Hamilton and thirteen sub-post offices located throughout the islands, which employ 179 people. Airmail departs and arrives daily (except on Sundays and public holidays) so that outgoing mail will be despatched the same day if received at the General Post Office in Hamilton by 9:30 am. Local mail is delivered twice daily and all post offices are open from 8:00 am to 5:00 pm Monday through Friday. As well, the General Post Office is open until noon on Saturdays. Mail for Europe, Africa, and the Middle East is routed through London; mail for Central and South America, Australia and the Far East is routed through New York. All international mail is carried by air but that with only surface stampage on it is not given priority treatment.

The value of philatelic sales from a small island was realised in the 1930s, using limited issues of attractive stamps which characterised Bermuda's unique qualities. Each year, three commemorative stamp series are issued and they are quickly bought by international stamp collectors. In fact, the Philatelic Bureau of the General Post Office has a mailing list and regularly fills orders for over 3,000 collectors.

Since 1979, Bermuda has developed express mail links with the postal administrations of the USA, UK, Canada, Brazil, Luxembourg, France, Switzerland, the Netherlands, and Sweden. Negotiations are in progress with authorities in Belgium, West Germany, and Hong Kong. Such mail is given overall priority which is geared to meet the requirements of Bermuda's international business community.

Telephone Service

Formed in 1886, ten years after the invention of the telephone, the Bermuda Telephone Company Limited is one of the world's oldest, continuously operating telephone organisations. Services began in July 1887 with one operator and twelve subscribers. By the third year of operation there were 140 subscribers, and by 1933 a fully automatic system was installed. As coaxial cables linked Bermuda with various other countries it was, by 1975, possible to dial directly to and from the USA, Canada, UK, Australia, France, West Germany, Hong Kong, Switzerland, eighteen Caribbean countries, and twenty-seven other countries. By 1982 all party lines in Bermuda were discontinued by which time there were 30,000 single lines. With the advent of digital technology Bermuda retired all the existing electromechanical exchanges and replaced them with electronic digital units; making Bermuda one of the first countries in the world to have a totally electronic switching network, with an initial capacity of 40,000 lines.

Cable and Wireless

All external communications for Bermuda are provided by Cable and Wireless Limited; these communications include among others: telephone (in conjunction with the Bermuda

Telephone Company), telex, packet-switching, facsimile, and telegraph. International telex is available to more than 180 destinations, 95 percent of which may be obtained automatically. Customers with letters, contracts, plans, and the like for overseas clients may use Telefax, a high-speed transmission service that utilizes the public telephone network. Telefax is also available in Bermuda to receive documents from overseas.

As the use of computers explodes, the demand for access to international databases and electronic mail has grown. Cable and Wireless International Database Access Service (IDAS) now provides access from Bermuda to Tymnet, Telenet, GEISCO, DATAPAC, ADP Autonet, Uninet, Transpac, and IPSS networks at speeds of 300bps or 1200bps; further enhancements are planned.

Since not every user requires a dedicated data link, the Cable and Wireless International Public Switched Data Service provides the facility to transmit data at 2,400bps on a time sensitive basis to the USA, UK, Canada, the Netherlands, Singapore, Barbados, and various other countries.

Financial and news agency services available in Bermuda and provided by Cable and Wireless include: Reuters' Rowgrabber Service, Reuters' MAT Service, Reuters' Monitor Service, AP-Dow Jones Telerate Service, AP-Dow Jones Quotron Service, Ap-Dow Jones Financial Wire Service, Reuters' News Service, and UPI News Service.

Telecommunications/Broadcasting

The Ministry of Industry and Technology is responsible for all aspects of telecommunications, broadcasting, and the development of new information-related industries for Bermuda. Particular main responsibilities are for: public broadcasting, public telecommunications services, land mobile radios, marine radio services, amateur radio, personal radio, aircraft radio, and frequency spectrum management. Many issues in the rapidly changing field are complex and not well understood so the Ministry is active in dealing with such things as electronic copyright, the renewal of Cable and Wireless' licence, computers in education, establishing

Bermuda as the hub in the development of transatlantic underseas cables, and exploring Bermuda's options in the direct broadcasting satellite field.

Prior to 1946 there was little broadcasting in Bermuda and local listeners relied on broadcasts originating in North America and England. However, the Bermuda Broadcasting Company was formed in 1943 and by 1946 was providing commercial radio with the call-sign ZBM on 1,240 kHz. A second station, ZBM-2 opened in 1962 when the power on both stations was increased to 1,000 watts with the inauguration of ZBM-FM. Capital Broadcasting, a second commercial company began ZFB in 1962 and then ZFB-FM in 1971. Finally, in 1981, a third company, St. George's Broadcasting Company opened VSB with an AM facility only.

ZBM-TV, Bermuda's first commercial television station, began operations in 1958 and a second station, Atlantic Broadcasting Company's ZFB-TV, initiated its programmes in 1965. In 1982, ZBM and ZFB radio and television merged operations to become the Bermuda Broadcasting Company Limited. The company has experienced labour disputes and temporary shutdown but, by 1984, there were 70,000 radio receivers and 35,000 television sets in use. It is also possible now to receive more channels by means of satellite dishes – some hotels, for example, offer sports networks.

Newspapers and Periodicals

The daily newspaper is *The Royal Gazette* which carries good coverage of world and local news. Weekly papers, such as the *Mid-Ocean News* and the *Bermuda Sun* provide similar services and are more lively than many weeklies found elsewhere. The monthly *The Bermudian* is a high quality magazine, and *This Week In Bermuda* is a weekly 100-page advertiser which is free and useful for tourists.

4 SOCIAL ENVIRONMENT

GOVERNMENT AND ADMINISTRATION

The Bermuda Parliament has been meeting in session since 1 August 1620 and, thus, is the oldest (not the first) legislative body overseas of the British Commonwealth. Bermuda, herself, being the oldest self-governing colony in the British Commonwealth. In fact, the Bermuda Parliament is third in age after the Parliaments in London and Iceland.

Since 1684 Governors of Bermuda have been appointed by the Crown and are now responsible for administration of justice, external affairs, internal security, the police, and defence. The Governor shares responsibility for police matters with the Minister of Home Affairs and, in most other instances, acts only on the advice of the Cabinet and/or his Council. In addition to the Governor, the Council includes the Premier and two or three Ministers. The Deputy Governor is the principal officer in the Governor's Office and, in the absence of the Governor, acts as Governor. Since neither the Crown, nor the Governor, have ultimate control of the Legislature it is a misnomer to speak of Bermuda as a Crown Colony, though that is sometimes done.

Constitution

The Bermuda Constitution came into effect in June 1968 and, as well as providing for internal self-government, it makes provisions for the protection of fundamental rights and freedoms of the individual and for the exercise of government through a legislature. The Legislature comprises two Houses of Parliament: the House of Assembly and the Senate (formerly called the Legislative Council). Parliament's functions are to pass laws regulating the life of the community; to make finance available for the needs of Government; to take formal action, cast in legislative form; and, to act as a forum for the public debate of issues of importance to the community. It is the custom that all proceedings of either House are public. The two Houses of Parliament are constituted on different principles and meet in different places, except on symbolic occasions such as the opening of Parliament, which is held in the Senate.

The House of Assembly

This body consists of forty Members of Parliament (MPs) who are elected under universal adult franchise from twenty constituencies. In turn, the MPs elect their own Speaker and Deputy Speaker. Eight of the parishes have two constituencies while Pembroke has four. Citizens are eligible to stand for election if they are British, have Bermuda Status, are 21 years old or more, and are ordinarily resident in Bermuda. Meetings of the House of Assembly take place on Fridays for approximately eight or nine months per year. The proceedings take place in a cool chamber with members facing each other across the benches and behaving decorously. If the political parties were evenly divided numerically, opponents would face each other. In practice at present, Government Members fill one side and take up ten seats on the other side.

In the 1968 and 1972 elections, the first under the new Constitution, thirty members were returned from the United Bermuda Party (UBP) and ten from the Progressive Labour Party (PLP). In subsequent elections the respective figures have been: 1976, UBP 25, PLP 15; 1980, UBP 22, PLP 18; 1983, UBP 26, PLP 14. Currently in 1986, and after a new party was formed in 1985, UBP holds 31 seats, PLP has 7, and the new National Liberal Party has 2.

The Senate

There are eleven members of the upper house, the Senate, of whom five are appointed on the advice of the Premier, three on the advice of the Opposition Leader, and three by the Governor. During Wednesday morning meetings through about nine months each year, the Senate usually deals with bills which have passed through the House of Assembly. However, Senate may initiate its own legislation except in the case of 'money bills'. The usual course of a bill is for the House of Assembly to initiate it, the Senate to approve it, and the Governor to sign it into statute. The circular table of the Senate Chamber, in the Cabinet Building, has also served many international gatherings including the Eisenhower-Churchill-Bidault 1953 'Three Power Conference', the 1957 Eisenhower-Macmillan meetings, and the meetings between Macmillan and Kennedy in 1961.

Each Parliament lasts five years or less and the Premier may ask the Governor to dissolve Parliament and call for a general election at any time.

The Premier

The Premier is the head of the Government and derives his unique position of authority from his majority in Parliament and from his sole right to appoint and discharge Cabinet Ministers. In addition to speaking on reserved subjects in the House and answering questions there, the Premier presides over Cabinet, generally supervises departments, and approves important departmental decisions which do not need to be considered by Cabinet. As well, the Premier makes recommendations to the Governor for appointments to boards, statutory commissions, and high judicial offices.

The Cabinet

Usually the Premier selects eleven Ministers to be Cabinet Members and he must have no fewer than six. Cabinet determines Government policies and then generally supervises the Government departments responsible for carrying out the policies. A Minister, as political head of a department, is responsible for all its acts and omissions so must bear the consequences of any dysfunctional consequences. The system is an effective way of bringing Government under public control.

Central Government finance is dealt with in Chapter 5.

The Cabinet Office

The Secretary to the Cabinet heads the Cabinet Office and the Public (Civil) Service. The Office operates under the authority or direction of the Premier to coordinate highest level policies. It prepares Cabinet agendas, circulates documents to Ministers, keeps minutes, monitors post-decisions' actions, and safeguards the security of documents. Additionally, the department is responsible for all personnel related matters in the Civil Service, management systems, public relations, protocol, business lotteries, and local Government services generally.

The Public Service Commission

The duties of the Public Service Commission are set out in the 1968 Bermuda Constitution but, broadly, its task is to ensure that candidates for the more senior public officer positions are selected for appointment on their merits and suitability alone. The five-person part-time Commission is appointed by the Governor, is independent, politically impartial, and responsible directly to the Governor.

Municipalities and Parishes

Hamilton (population 2,000), which boasts one of the finest sheltered harbours in the world, was incorporated in 1790 and became the capital of Bermuda in 1815. By an act of legislation it was made a city in 1897 and is governed by a Corporation. Its main sources of revenue are from municipal taxes and from charges for waterfront and dock facilities. The original capital and only other municipality, St. George's (population 1,600), is one of the oldest settlements in the western hemisphere. It also gains its revenue from municipal taxes and waterfront facilities.

Prior to 1971, the nine parishes elected their own vestries with the power to levy taxes and manage local affairs. However, in 1971, the Government replaced the vestries with nominated and largely advisory parish councils. Incidentally, the City of Hamilton is in Pembroke Parish and not Hamilton Parish.

Boards and Committees

About 100 boards and committees, served by approximately 1,000 members, help to ensure the smooth and effective running of Government departments. Members, who comprise a mixture of ages, sexes, races, religions, and experiences, may apply for their positions and are selected by the Governor, the Premier, and Cabinet Ministers.

LAW AND ORDER

The laws in Bermuda are based on English common law, which includes principles of equity, and all English Acts of general application that were in force on 11 July 1612. However, these laws of principles are subject to Bermudian acts, which have been passed since 1612, to repeal, modify, or amend them. The Public Acts passed by the Bermuda Legislature, and Statutory Instruments made under them, are contained in the loose-leaf bound 'Revised Laws of Bermuda'. Additionally there is a two-volume edition of private acts covering the period 1709–1953. Since 1953, private acts have been published in annual volumes.

The Judiciary

The Chief Justice heads the Judicial Department and, along with puisne judges and magistrates, is appointed by the Governor. Bermuda has a three-tier court system consisting of the Magistrates' Court (the lower court), the Supreme Court (or high court), and the Court of Appeal. The latter is made up of a President, three Justices of Appeal, and a Registrar. It sits three times each year to hear appeals from decisions of the Supreme Court. Appeals from this court go to the Judicial Committee of the United Kingdom Privy Council, which is the final avenue of appeal.

The Bermuda Supreme Court, which consists of the Chief Justice and three puisne judges, exercises unlimited jurisdiction in all divisions of the law. It sits all the year round to hear and make decisions on criminal, divorce, and civil matters. All the Court's criminal trials have juries. Also, the Supreme Court hears appeals from the Magistrates' Court.

The Magistrates' Court of Bermuda is headed by a senior magistrate and has two other magistrates serving on it. The magistrates sit in Hamilton but they have jurisdiction throughout Bermuda. They conduct trials without juries and have jurisdiction over all summary offences. As well, with the consent of the accused, they may deal with certain indictable offences. Magistrates' duties also include work on family disputes, juvenile offences, and as coroners. In Coroner's Court the Magistrate hears inquests into cases of accidental death and into the causes of fires. Magistrates also chair quasi-judicial statutory tribunals, such as the Liquor Licensing Authority.

Police Services

Though the Governor has direct responsibility for the Police Service he has, since 1977, delegated responsibility for recruitment, staffing, general organisation, finance, and community relations to the Minister of Home Affairs. At the end of 1985 the authorized size of the Bermuda Police Force was 453 men and women. The Service is under the command of a Commissioner, who is aided by a Deputy Commissioner and two Assistant Commissioners. Each of the Service's five divisions – Headquarters, Central, Eastern, Western, and Operations – is commanded by an Inspector or Chief Inspector. And, the Criminal Investigation Department, commanded by an Assistant Commissioner, includes a Special Branch and a Narcotics Section.

The Operations Division maintains motorised traffic patrols, garages, workshops, and radio communications contacts with all motor, foot, emergency, and marine patrols. The latter uses its four craft to patrol inland waters and harbours so as to enforce marine regulations, protect small islands' property, and to detect or prevent crime on the water.

Training police officers continues to improve at the Police Training School where courses cover the 15-week basic training, localisation, recruits' refresher courses, CID aides, overseas recruits' orientation, and pre-promotion tuition. Preparation in specialised areas such as narcotics enforcement, crime investigation, marine searches, and police administration is often obtained by sending officers to training establishments in Canada, the US, and the UK. It is interesting to see, however, that Bermudianisation of the police force is being enhanced by the Police Cadet Scheme which is carried out in collaboration with the Bermuda College.

The fight against crime has intensified as the police struggle to combat the importation and use of illicit drugs. Cannabis, heroin, and cocaine all find their way to Bermuda from diverse parts of the world. This has led much of the islands' crime – notably thefts and burglaries – to be drug related. Crimes of violence are not uncommon but, thankfully, they seldom involve firearms because of the strict gun control measures. Also, the police service remains an unarmed body. Crime prevention aided the police in actively maintaining good relations with the general public. For example, they maintain an Outward Bound scheme, have Junior Police Cadets, a pedal cycle gymkhana for children, and officers are involved with Sea Cadets, Scouts, sports coaching and other youth activities. Additionally, the Neighbourhood Watch Scheme and the U-mark programme have gained increasing support and shown good results.

To give an idea of the scale of crime, the approximate value of property stolen during 1983 was $1,841,648 and police investigations led to the recovery of $500,011. That year police investigated 5,049 indictable crimes of which 4,831 proved to be true cases. As a result, 1,212 persons were convicted – a record which compares favourably with many of the world's police forces.

Traffic duty also keeps the police force busy. In 1983, speeding, alcohol, and generally careless driving resulted in 3,430 road accidents and seventeen fatalities. Given the circumstances, these numbers were quite unacceptable for the future so extensive media campaigns were launched on the issue of road safety and other more direct controls were invoked. As a result, in 1984, monthly accidents dropped from 285 to 252 and the number of deaths dropped from seventeen to four.

Prisons

Bermuda's Ministry of Health and Social Services has responsibility for the four prisons – Casemates, at Ireland Island (men's maximum security); the minimum security Prison Farm at Ferry Reach, St. George's; the Senior Training School (for youths 16–20 years); and, the Women's Prison (for adults and girls). The system is administered, from Prison Headquarters on the outskirts of Hamilton, by a Commissioner of Prisons who heads a staff of 168, including 110 prison officers. The number of people incarcerated has declined over the past few years but those who remain in are there for longer terms. About one-third of the prisoners are in for drug related offences and one-third for theft or breaking and entering. Recently, three people were serving life sentences for murder and four were serving time for manslaughter – thus reflecting the infrequency of such serious crimes in Bermuda.

Remarkable efforts are made in Bermuda to look after prisoners' health and welfare while they are in prison and to rehabilitate them in preparation for release. So much so, that locals say that people have been known to break into Bermuda's prisons for shelter, good food, and recreational facilities!

Fire Services

Local government fire protection began in Hamilton in 1840 when six 'leathern buckets' were bought in New York by a councillor and six more were ordered in England. Then, in 1842, another 100 buckets were purchased! With these humble beginnings, fire protection remained with volunteers until 1961 when a full-time crew was formed. In 1983, the brigade was taken over from the Corporation of Hamilton by the Bermuda Government – though volunteers still assist the full-time personnel. Now, the Bermuda Fire Service is responsible for fire coverage on the islands except at St. George's and at the US Bases. St. George's brigade is still successfully manned by about thirty volunteers and one paid mechanic under the direction of the Corporation of St. George's. In the west end there is a sub-station in Sandys Parish which can receive back-up support from the Central

Station. Indeed, all the services in Bermuda have arrangements to assist each other when needs arise.

EDUCATION

Though having a North American influence, the Bermuda Government's educational services are generally guided by the British system and include the commitment to try to develop each person into a sound, fully functioning adult and effective citizen. Equal educational opportunities are available for everyone and the Government spends about 17 percent of its annual budget on these purposes. Children must attend school from age five through sixteen years and they receive the education without paying fees. Pre-school nurseries are also free for four-year-olds, although there are some fee-paying nurseries. And, of course, fees are charged at private schools.

Most of Bermuda's schools are co-educational but two Government-funded single-sex schools, and private all boys' and all girls' schools, are available. There are no boarding schools. At the end of 1985 there were 10,589 pupils in the schools with 8,163 of them in Government schools, 1,876 in private schools, and 550 at the Bermuda College (plus approximately 2,000 part-time students at the College). The students are taught by close to 1,000 teachers of whom nearly two-thirds are Bermudians, while the remainder come from the UK, Canada, the West Indies, and the USA. Pupil/teacher ratios are about 1 to 17 in primary schools and 1 to 12 in secondary schools.

The islands have eleven nurseries, eighteen primary schools, fourteen secondary schools (of which five are private), and four special schools which cater for blind, deaf, speech impaired, and multiple disabled children. As well, there is an Opportunity Workshop for severely handicapped people aged between fourteen and twenty-one years. All schools try to involve parents in their children's education through PTAs and other means throughout the three-term forty-week school year.

The Department of Education

The general administration of education is the responsibility of the Minister of Education who is assisted by a permanent secretary and an advisory Board of Education. The Department's role is divided into four segments dealing with curriculum and instruction, administration and personnel, special services, and pupil services.

Primary Education

Children usually attend primary schools in their own geographical areas until they are eleven or twelve years of age, when they transfer to secondary schools. In these primary years the schools try to help all children to communicate effectively; to acquire permanent literacy and numeracy skills; to begin to think scientifically and logically; to demonstrate a knowledge and awareness of civics as a basis for future participation in, and contribution to, the life of the society; to develop manipulative skills, artistic talents, physical abilities, and to cultivate good health habits. Thus, a general system-wide curriculum includes English, mathematics, physical education, social studies, art, and music.

Secondary Education

During the secondary school years students are taught appropriate attitudes and job entry level prerequisites; and, to show tolerance, respect, and the ability to form responsible relations with people in social, cultural, and ethnic groups which are different from their own. Emphasis is placed on students acquiring habits, attitudes, and values associated with responsible citizenship and the preservation of Bermuda's physical environment. As well, particular attention is paid to students acquiring an understanding of ethical principles and values, and on being able to apply them in everyday life.

More specifically, curricula are designed to help each student to develop higher level competencies in reading, writing, and mathematics; to acquire a basic stock of factual information concerning the principles of physical, biological, and social sciences; and, to have familiarity with the historical record of human achievements and failures, as well as with current social issues. When they leave school, the students are meant to be able to demonstrate that they have acquired the knowledge, ability, and desire necessary for further education and lifelong learning. And, that they know their own worth, abilities, and potentialities.

All this is implemented by means of the five-year Bermuda Secondary School Curriculum (BSSC) through the successful completion of which leads to the award of the BSSC certificate. As well, depending on curricula emphases chosen, students may take external examinations such as the University of London General Certificate (GCE), the Associate Examining Board GCE, and examinations of the Pitman Institute, the Royal School of Music, and the Royal Society of Arts.

Post Secondary Education

The islands have only one tertiary education institution – The Bermuda College. It was formed in 1974 by amalgamating the Bermuda Technical Institute, the Hotel and Catering College, and the Academic Sixth Form Centre. Within the College the earlier units initially became the Department of Commerce and Technology, the Department of Hotel Technology, and the Department of Academic Studies. However, when the Stonington Beach Hotel (see below) was added in 1980, the College established five departments as follows: Academic Studies, Business Studies, Hotel Technology, Technology, and General Studies.

As a community college, the Bermuda College tries to respond to the educational and training needs of local people and is flexible in meeting the ever-changing demands for skilled workers. With tourism being Bermuda's main industry, high priority is given to providing business training skills and the expertise required in the hospitality industry. But, the College also includes the academic apex of the local educational system and, as such, provides the first two years of undergraduate instruction which can transfer abroad and lead to a bachelor's degree from recognised universities. As well, in the field of adult education, the College offers full- and part-time extension courses for general education, occupational training, and the leisure pursuits of adults. Also, extension courses of the University of Maryland and Queen's University (Canada) are available through the College.

In the Department of Hotel Technology courses are given in accommodation studies, cookery, food sanitation, waiting, beverage services, tourism, and public relations. The Stonington Beach Hotel, situated on its own beach with many fine tourist facilities, provides excellent opportunities for in-service training. The hotel is run as a business operation and the students are required by their instructors to provide top quality services for the paying guests.

Alternative Educational Opportunities

First, the Adult Education School is a privately operated school which receives an annual grant from the Government through the Bermuda College. The School has adopted an individualised, non-formal approach to providing academic upgrading, retraining, developmental reading, and English as a second language. Some students take the SET and GED examinations so as to qualify for college entrance and teaching is by the Laubach principle of 'each one teach one' – using volunteer instructors.

Secondly, students who do seek further education receive considerable financial assistance from the Government, from the private sector, and from the UK Government (in fee differential grants). Generally, funds are available when programmes are not available in Bermuda and when the qualification sought is relevant to the needs of the Bermuda community. In a recent typical year 1,000 Bermuda residents were studying in the USA, over 400 were in Canada, 146 in the UK, and 24 were in the West Indies.

HEALTH SERVICES

Standards of health and social care provided by Government and private practitioners are high in Bermuda. The Ministry of Health and Social Services commands the largest single portion of the entire Government budget – approximately 23 percent. The Department of Health is responsible for the public health of Bermuda, disease prevention, and health promotion services through the following programmes.

Personal and Dental Health

For the most part, personal and dental health services are offered free of charge to Bermuda residents. Doctors, dentists, and nurses at the Victoria Street Branch provide personal health services and separate programmes exist for family planning, ante-natal, post-natal, and gynaecological care. Children subsequently receive routine preventive health care in such areas as developmental assessments, immunizations, hearing and vision screening.

At the adult level the Department provides comprehensive medical care for the police, prison officers, and prisoners while, more generally, programmes exist in community services which cover such areas as health education, nutrition, speech, language, and hearing rehabilitation. For the elderly, home health care services include nursing, therapeutic, and personal care services.

The Disease Surveillance Unit is responsible for epidemiologic surveillance and the investigation of communicable diseases. Issues relating to food hygiene, airport hygiene sanitation, airport quarantine, air pollution, water pollution, water quality, and occupational health are all the responsibility of the Environmental Health section. The Public Health Laboratory identifies and confirms all public health hazards; analyses water and food for bacteriological, mineral, and organic impurities; and, analyses and identifies drugs and toxic substances.

All medical and dental practitioners are in private practice and their fees are similar to those found in North America. Visitors who require a doctor or dentist can usually obtain one through their hotel or guest house.

Hospitals

The only general hospital on the islands is the King Edward VII Memorial Hospital (KEMH) which is operated, using Government funds, by the Bermuda Hospitals' Board (appointed by the Minister). The hospital, which has 223 beds, is accredited by the Canadian Council on Hospital Accreditation. It is modern, fully-equipped, air-conditioned and generally a fine facility. A portion of an older wing has been renovated so it can now accommodate ninety-two geriatric and rehabilitation patients.

KEMH has over 200 registered nurses, thirty enrolled nurses, twelve resident doctors, and about fifty doctors on the attending staff. There are specialists and consultants in anaesthesiology, gerontology, internal medicine, obstetrics and gynaecology, opthalmology, orthopaedics, otolaryngology, paediatrics, pathology, psychiatry, radiology, surgery, and urology. There is an excellent emergency department which is staffed twenty-four hours a day and four ambulances are stationed at the hospital.

Mentally ill patients are cared for at St. Brendan's Hospital, which is also administered through the Bermuda Hospitals' Board. It has 175 beds together with in-patient facilities, out-patient clinics, an occupational therapy department, and a recreational therapy department. Apart from the nursing and administrative staff, St. Brendan's can call on four consultant psychiatrists and four mental welfare officers.

Health Insurance Plans

The Hospital Insurance Plan (HIP) is available to all employed and self-employed persons and their non-employed spouses. The HIP Act (1971) makes hospital insurance available to all residents of Bermuda irrespective of their age or state of health. The Act also provides free hospital care for school children up to sixteen years of age and for full-time students in Bermuda up to the age of twenty-one. There is also a Government Employees' Health Insurance Scheme which is mandatory for all Government employees, the non-employed spouses of Government employees and their children. Most private businesses and public utilities have contributory health insurance schemes which are usually operated through private insurance companies.

SOCIAL SERVICES

Bermuda's first Director of Social Services was appointed in 1972 shortly after the passing of the Social Welfare Act. The Act defined social welfare as 'denoting desirable standards or conditions of moral or physical well-being.' Since then, a number of programmes have developed which include the following services.

Day Care Centre

The Government Day Care Centre opened in the early seventies on Happy Valley Road in Pembroke with the specific intent of catering for families in that area. It can accommodate up to fifty children, aged three months to four years, who have economic and other needs for specialised day care attention.

Residential Care

There are four residential units of which three are for young people. Most admissions for young people result from Court orders, although a few children are placed there voluntarily by their parents or guardians. The adult facility, known as Reachout Rehabilitation Community, takes males over sixteen years and offers job preparation counselling, personal counselling, and an opportunity to improve basic educational skills.

Family Services

For the most part, Family Services provides child welfare services in the areas of child abuse, child neglect, custody, adoption, foster care, and general counselling.

Social Assistance

Individuals who can demonstrate their inability to meet their financial requirements for basic necessities are given financial assistance. Payments are made through parish councils after social assistance workers have made their assessments.

The Elderly

The Department employs a person to coordinate social service programmes for the aged and handicapped. Services include community assessment in preparation for providing more comprehensive in-home help, or for placement in a geriatric facility.

Over the years Lefroy House, a former children's home, became first a retirement facility and later a nursing home which now has seventy beds. Its purpose is to provide nursing care, health supervision, and rehabilitation services to patients aged over sixty-five years.

Probation Services

Probation Services form that part of the Department which assists the Court by advising, assisting, and befriending persons who have been placed on probation.

Grants and Contributions

To help improve the social well-being of Bermudians, the Department grants approximately $3 million per year to community organizations such as Teen Services, Hope Homes, The Salvation Army, Parish Rest Homes, the Meals-on-Wheels Association, Legal Aid, the Marriage Guidance Council, and Beacon House (which cares for blind people).

Department of Social Insurance

In addition to a contributory old age pension and a widow's allowance, the Contributory Pensions Act 1967 provides a non-contributory pension to residentially qualified sixty-five year olds and, since 1980, has provided disability benefits.

PUBLIC WORKS

The Department of Public Works is responsible for the design, construction, maintenance, and improvement of all public works, public buildings, public water supply, sewage schemes, highways, bridges, and the collection and disposal of solid wastes. The Department employs over twenty professionals, sixty other staff, and an industrial force of more than 400 craftsmen and labourers.

Roads

Bermuda has approximately 200 km (125 miles) of paved public highways and about 215 km (135 miles) of mostly-paved private estate roads. Road signs observe international conventions and the speed limit is 35 kph (21.9 mph), except in St. George's where the limit is 25 kph (15 mph).

With the recent replacement of the Watford Bridge by a new steel/composite concrete deck structure and the rebuilding of Somerset Bridge, the main road link between Hamilton and the Dockyard is now free of weight restrictions for standard highway vehicles. However, a ten-ton restriction remains on the Swing Bridge route into St. George's.

Buildings and Land

The Department was responsible for constructing the new Government Administration Building on Parliament Street which opened in 1980 to house numerous departments from Archives through Tax Commissioner. Works have also recently included extensive docks' renovations, schools' additions, hospital redevelopments, golf course construction, and the building of the women's prison. Altogether, the Government's estate comprises some 750 entities ranging from houses and office buildings through schools to major complexes such as those for police, prisons, the Civil Air Terminal, and Bermuda College. The total insured value of the properties is in the region of $300 million which is 75 percent of their replacement value. As well, the Government carries public liability insurance which gives it indemnity up to $6 million for any one event.

The provision of land for Government purposes receives ongoing attention. Recent major acquisitions have mainly centred on recreational requirements, nature reserves, and road improvements. Revised maps of Bermuda on the scales 1:2500 and 1:10,560, which for the first time incorporate road names and numbers, have been prepared for the Department and are on sale to the general public.

Water Works

The Government has an advantageous operating agreement

with the Watlington Waterworks which calls for the supply to consumers of over 220 million gallons of central lens water annually at a price of $8.50 per 1,000 gallons. Also, more wells have been drilled throughout the central lens region in order to spread the abstraction over as wide an area as possible. The Water Authority authorises the abstraction of over one million gallons of water per day from the 150 wells.

To supplement the water supply a reverse osmosis plant at St. Brendan's Hospital produces close to 400,000 gallons per day and other plants are in various stages of development. The Government continues to define, quantify, and monitor the available groundwater resources using a mini-computer mathematical model to assist in the tasks. It is intended to develop other lenses in Warwick and Southampton as needs arise.

Refuse

The Government collects refuse from households twice weekly and then has the problem of appropriate disposal. In 1974 a refuse pulverisation plant was installed for the purpose of homogenisation and reduction in size of all suitable garbage prior to it being used as fill material in a marsh reclamation scheme. However, improved technology is always needed and the Government is currently constructing a new refuse incinerator and waste treatment plant, with heat recovery and power generation facilities, to replace the pulverisation plant.

ELECTRICITY SUPPLY

The Bermuda Electric Light Company Limited, a privately owned company with about 1,000 shareholders, generates and distributes electric power throughout Bermuda – except at the US Naval Air Station at Kindley Field which has its own generating capacity. A new Systems Control and Data Acquisition process is operational that includes twenty-one Remote Terminal Units. All supply network information is received and processed by the dual system with automatic failover computers. The computers' storage capacity is such that, ultimately, the total company systems of generation, transmission, and distribution will be constantly supervised and an instantaneous alarm will be given for any malfunction.

THE ARMED FORCES

The governments of four countries – Bermuda, Canada, UK, USA – maintain military installations in Bermuda.

Bermuda Regiment

Under the Bermuda Constitution, the Governor commands the Bermuda Regiment after receiving advice from the Defence Board. The Regiment's main responsibility is to watch over internal security and assist the Police in maintaining law and order. The force now numbers 650 and each year a computer ballot takes place for conscription and involves all Bermudian males aged eighteen and nineteen. One hundred and eighty new recruits are needed each year of whom sixty are taken as volunteers while 120 enter via the conscription ballot for the compulsory three years of service. The permanent staff includes five British Army officers and warrant officers on secondment, together with seventeen Bermudian officers, warrant officers, and non-commissioned officers (NCOs). Three NCOs are servicewomen and many appropriate positions are being most successfully filled by women. It first became possible for them to join the forces in 1979.

The Regiment is organised into four companies and support groups – two rifle companies, one training company, and a headquarters company. Each year the two rifle companies, with elements of support personnel, take part in overseas training exercises in such locations as the UK, the US, and Canada. Often, support is provided by the Jamaican Defence Force, training is given by the US Marines, and the Regiment enjoys an alliance with the Lincoln and Welland Regiment in Canada. It is also affiliated with the Royal Anglian Regiment in England.

Apart from overseas training, the Regiment has a 15-day annual camp and regular drill periods throughout the year. As well, it provides ceremonial guards of honour for the Governor and visiting dignitaries, and takes part in ceremonial parades.

HMS Malabar

The UK no longer maintains a strong presence in Bermuda having decommissioned most of its fortress in the 1950s. Now, the British presence is maintained by the Senior British Officer, Bermuda, and the staff at HMS *Malabar* at Freeport. They handle incoming RN ships and perform some ceremonial duties.

United States Navy

The US has the largest foreign forces presence in Bermuda. Its Naval Air Station on St. David's Island property was created in the early 1940s from several small islands in Castle Harbour which were linked by land-fill. The site also serves as the Civil Air Terminal and the same air traffic equipment is used by both segments.

Additionally, the US has a Naval Annex in Southampton Parish which is commissioned to maintain and operate facilities needed by aviation units and other activities of the US Navy.

Canadian Forces

The US Naval Annex also houses the Liaison Office of the Canadian Forces which handles incoming Canadian ships, aircraft, and visiting forces. Canadian military exercises are conducted throughout the year and the Office also carries out some consular activities on behalf of the Canadian High Commission to Bermuda, which is located in New York. As well, at Daniel's Head, Sandys Parish, the Canadian Forces operate a communications and research station. The forces personnel participate in local sea rescues and in ceremonial occasions.

5 ECONOMY

Bermuda's geographical location, its climate, and its people are its only natural resources and so, throughout history, the islands' economic base has changed to reflect the influences of local phenomena and international economic trends. In the early years, cedar was abundant and formed a basis for the principal industry of ship building, which, together with the salt trade, were the foundations of Bermuda's economy. For a while during the late 1800s and early 1900s, fresh vegetables were exported from the islands to the northeastern United States until, in 1920 a protective tariff was enacted in the US which ended the enterprise. With no raw materials, Bermuda has had to depend on its most valuable resource of people to capitalise on the geographical location and develop its industries. Today, Bermuda's economy is based mainly on two principal service industries – first, and of prime importance, is tourism and second is international company business. It is recognised that the well-being and prosperity of the two major means of livelihood are determined to a large extent by external factors. Bermuda relies on the United States for 85 percent of its visitors so, of course, recession, inflation, and other economic factors in that country can have a marked influence on Bermuda's economy.

In this chapter particular emphasis is on tourism and international business but other economic and financial activity is reviewed.

GENERAL REVIEW

When Bermuda's Minister of Finance made his Budget Statement for 1986–87 he was cautiously optimistic for the future. Bermuda's Gross Domestic Product, in current dollars, had grown by 13 percent in 1982–83, by 11 percent in 1983–84, and at the end of that financial year Bermuda became a billion dollar economy for the first time. Bermuda ranks among the top ten countries in the world with a per capita income in excess of $18,000 per annum and there is no national debt.

Of course economic growth in the United States, the value of the dollar, overseas inflation, world interest rates, and oil prices all affect Bermuda's economy. Importantly, the value of the US dollar fell in the year leading up to 1986–87 by 15 percent on average against the other major currencies. Such a change has a direct bearing on the price of Bermuda's services, expressed in foreign currencies, thus tilting the competitive balance back in Bermuda's favour. However, to consolidate this type of advantage it is essential that prices in Bermuda do not rise to offset the gain. In particular, those providing services for tourists and international companies need, wherever possible, to hold prices at their 1985 levels.

Bermuda should be greatly assisted in keeping its inflation level at 3.5 percent if world disinflation continues. For example, in 1985, consumer price inflation was 3.6 percent in the US, 2 percent in Japan, and 4.5 percent (on average) in Europe. Although other factors have played a part in the decline in inflation since 1980, the drop in commodity prices by some 30 percent has been most important. It may be unrealistic for Bermuda to expect further reductions in commodity prices with one important exception. Oil prices have fallen sharply and, if crude oil prices remain at $20 a barrel or below, then the effect on inflation, interest rates, and economic growth in the developed economies (including Bermuda's) will be nothing but good.

The US budget deficit encompasses political and economic problems. If it is not reduced interest rates are likely to rise and lead to some recession in the US economy as consumer spending, investment, and stockbuilding decline. Such eventualities would possibly hurt Bermuda.

When the Minister made his 1986–87 Budget Statement, full and final information was not available on the 1985–86 year. However, Bermuda's economy as measured in terms of GDP (i.e. output adjusted for price movement) had weakened in 1984–85. There was a fall in tourist spending of about 3 percent in real terms, a sharp increase in imports, and no growth in exports, thus suggesting that the economy was at best flat. The balance of payments, though, did appear to have shown some improvement on the previous year's deficit of $21 million. But it is too early to say whether the improvement will have been sufficient to return the balance of payments to the surplus of 1985.

Government expenditures for 1986–87 were planned to increase 7.8 percent over the previous year to be $200.7 million on the current account and $30.7 million for capital projects. The major spending ministries were Health and Social Services $44.2 million (22 percent), Education $34.6 million (17.2 percent), Labour and Home Affairs $24.9 million (12.4 percent), Finance $24 million (12 percent), Works and Housing $21.4 million (10.7 percent), and Tourism $19.4 million (9.7 percent). In preparing to cover the expenditures, the Minister assumed: (1) that the number of regular visitors would increase by 7 percent and therefore produce more revenue; (2) the number of cruise passengers would decline slightly; (3) international company expenditures would show no growth; (4) rising real incomes would provide a further boost to consumers' expenditures and thus, generally, domestic demand would grow; and, (5) imports would rise in dollar terms by 2 percent. Overall, the real GDP was expected to grow by 2 percent in 1986–87 and this would only be feasible if some minor changes in taxes and fees were made. The Minister proposed to make changes in vehicle licence fees, land taxes, customs duties, and a variety of other areas.

MINISTRY OF FINANCE

The Ministry of Finance Headquarters is directed by a Financial Secretary and comprises an Economic Adviser, an Assistant Financial Secretary in charge of the Budget Office, and six support staff. The principal functions of the Headquarters' staff are to advise the Minister on policy issues, to prepare briefings, draft speeches, oversee Ministry departments, and to monitor and control Government revenues and expenditures.

Accountant General's Department
The Accountant General is responsible for the collection of Government revenue and the disbursement of Government expenditures, together with the management of the Government's financial assets and liabilities. The Department also maintains the Government's central accounting records, operates the Government Employee Health Insurance scheme, and provides advisory data to other sectors.

Central Data Processing
The Central Data Processing Department's staff of thirty-seven provides its services to all Government departments and is responsible for the provision of office automation together with distributed processing facilities. Regular tasks cover all aspects of Government activity and the staff is currently engaged in a five-year systems plan to bring interactive computing facilities to nearly all Government departments.

Department of Management Services
Management Services acts in an advisory and consulting capacity encompassing organisational/staffing reviews, work and method studies, systems and procedure evaluation, and small-scale data processing. The Department is also responsible for coordinating and implementing special projects in close cooperation with the departments concerned.

Personnel Services
The Personnel Services section of the Ministry deals with a myriad of Government programmes and services which include: advice on personnel and industrial relations, collective agreement negotiations, staff recruitment, staff development, and maintaining central personnel records.

Statistical Department

Responsibility for the collection and publication of economic, social, and demographic statistics falls to the Statistical Department. To such ends the Department carries out special studies, surveys, and a population census every ten years. During the most recent census in 1980, every houshold in Bermuda was included to provide the most comprehensive profile of the islands' population ever stored on computer tape, thus allowing easy access to the raw data so that cross tabulations by any of the characteristics collected can be obtained. In 1982, a Household Expenditure survey was carried out in a sample of almost 500 households to obtain detailed income and expenditure data ranging from the amounts spent on newspapers to expenditures on major kitchen appliances. The purpose being to update the weighting pattern employed in the construction of the Retail Price Index and to determine updated income distribution estimates.

In general terms, the Department's long-range goals are to provide a wider range of key data that are accurate, timely, and relevant to the social and economic development of Bermuda. In this context it is intended that the scope of social statistics be broadened with a view to widening the community's knowledge about the quality of life in the islands. Additionally, it is intended to extend the National Accounts by developing sector accounts, and to establish two more indices – a construction price index and an office supplies price index.

The Monetary Authority

The Authority is responsible for the issue and redemption of Bermuda currency, monitoring the performance of local banks, the supervision of deposit companies, the regulation of interest and credit charges, the administration of exchange control, the compilation and interpretation of balance of payment statistics, the vetting of applications for the incorporation of local and exempted companies, and acting as advisor to Government on banking and monetary matters. As a Government-owned corporation, the Authority is operated

Visitors' transportation. Many visitors to Bermuda move around on hired mopeds

Mr. Speaker. MPs elect their own Speaker. In this picture is the Hon. F. John Barritt, Speaker of the House of Assembly

Housebuilding rates remain high in Bermuda. Here the characteristic roofs are under construction

Quiet Beaches. An attractive feature for tourists is the Bermuda shoreline which has a large number of secluded beaches from small ones like this to one which is two miles long

Somerset Bridge connects the Bermuda mainland with Somerset Island and is believed to be the smallest drawbridge in the world

by a board of directors which is appointed by the Minister of Finance.

In 1982, the Authority put in general circulation the $100 note which carries on it two small dots that allow the sight impaired to distinguish the note's value by touch. Coins valued at $5 and $1 were brought out in 1983 and, to mark the occasion, a proof set of all of Bermuda's circulation coinage was produced. Enhanced attractiveness for collectors was ensured by limiting the number of sets to 10,000. When the Prince of Wales married Lady Diana Spencer, the Authority commemorated the event by minting its largest denomination gold coin valued at $250. Also, a $1 silver coin was made available, and all such coins may now be bought at local dealers.

Generally, the currency of the islands is the Bermuda dollar which has the same value as the US dollar. Currency notes are issued in denominations of $100, $50, $20, $10, $5, and $1 (cupro-nickel), 50 cents, 25 cents, 10 cents, 5 cents (cupro-nickel), and 1 cent (bronze). US dollars are generally accepted in shops and hotels though that is not now the situation with Canadian dollars. Further, pounds sterling ceased to be redeemed by the Monetary Authority in 1980.

Audit Department

The Auditor's function is to audit and express a professional opinion on the accounts of the Senate, the House of Assembly, all courts, and all Government departments and offices. The Department's Annual Report is submitted to the Governor, the Speaker of the House of Assembly, and the President of the Senate who all lay the report before their respective bodies. Importantly, under the Constitution, the Auditor is not subject to the direction of any person or authority when exercising official functions.

TAXATION

Bermuda is a low tax jurisdiction with modest rates when compared with most developed countries of the world. There are no personal nor corporate income taxes, and there is no capital gains tax. In fact, 43 percent of revenue for the

Government comes from customs duties while other sources of revenue include payroll taxes, company fees, land taxes, stamp duties, and a variety of minor taxes and fees.

Customs Duties

Generally, duties in Bermuda are calculated on an *ad valorem* basis on the value of imported goods. The normal rate is 20 percent although many food items are exempt and lower rates apply to certain essentials and materials used in local manufacturing. Certain luxury items, such as boats and television sets, incur duty at 30 percent while duties on alcohol, cigarettes, and petroleum are levied on a specific basis. The highest duty of 55 percent is on cars and car parts. The most visible presence of customs officers, so far as the general public is concerned, is at the airport where about sixty staff examine commercial shipments arriving by air. As well, customs services are provided in St. George's Harbour.

Another facet of the Customs Service's responsibilities is that of being the first line of defence against the intrusion of undesirable persons and goods, so as to help to safeguard the social and economic well-being of the islands.

Principal imports to Bermuda are foodstuffs, liquor, clothing, furniture, fuel, electrical appliances, and motor vehicles. Main exports are pharmaceuticals, concentrates, essences, and liquor. The total revenue expected from duties in 1986–87 is $97.59 million. This is out of a total anticipated revenue of $231,508,700.

Hospital Levy

The hospital levy must be paid by all employers, including international companies, at a rate of 4 percent of payrolls. The employer may recover half of the tax from employees. The tax paid by international companies is not assessed on actual payrolls but at 4 percent of a flat $21,000 per employee. Churches, charities, schools, Government, and parish councils pay at 1.5 percent of payrolls and can withhold the full amount from their employees' remuneration. This levy, it is anticipated, will produce 11.45 percent of the total 1986–87 Government revenue.

Employment Tax

A tax of 5 percent is normally charged on the total of an employer's payroll after the inclusion of the value of fringe benefits. A national assessment is made in respect of the labour element in the income of self-employed persons. International companies, registered charities, and public bodies are not liable to the tax and exemptions are given to such individuals as farmers, taxi drivers, and commercial fishermen. Employers with a payroll of less than $36,000 are also exempt from the tax. Hotels and restaurants pay employment tax at 2 percent, though hotels are not liable for the tax during the three months of December through February. This tax is expected to produce 8.94 percent of the Government's total revenue in 1986–87.

Company Taxes and Fees

International companies pay a fee on incorporation and annually thereafter, the rate being $2,250 for insurance companies (excluding insurance management and brokerage) and mutual funds/finance companies and £1.200 for insurance management/brokerage and all other types of companies. Insurance companies must also pay a one-time registration fee and an annual business fee. For insurance companies, excluding management or brokerage companies, the fees are respectively $2,000 and $1,500 per year. For insurance management/brokerage companies, the corresponding fees are $1,000 and $500 per year.

Local companies pay an annual tax which varies from $500 to $5,000 depending on the amount of their issued capital. Banks and deposit companies also pay annual licence fees of $25,000 and $1,500 respectively. Real estate agents pay $100 on the issuance and renewal of licences and a fee of $10 is payable on the issuance and annual renewal of a real estate salesperson's licence. Foreign owned companies, in which Bermudian interest is less than 60 percent, also pay a fee on issue of a licence and $1,000 annually. All these fees and taxes are expected to produce 5.36 percent of Government revenues in 1986–87.

Land Tax

All Bermudian property except undeveloped land, Crown land, and land owned by local governments, charitable organisations, schools, foreign governments, and certain other properties, is subject to a tax on an assessed annual rental value (ARV). Prior to 1986–87, commercial property taxes' annual rates were 3.6 percent of their ARV, while private dwellings, were taxed on a scale rising from 1.25 percent on properties with an ARV of up to $7,200 to 6.5 percent on properties with an annual value of more than $36,000. During 1986–87 all rates were increased by 5 percent so as to yield an additional half a million dollars per year. Owner-occupiers, aged 65 years or more, may deduct from their unit's ARV the sum of $20,000 and apply to the resultant amount the appropriate tax percentage. This source is expected to yield 4.69 percent of 1986–87 Government revenues.

Hotel Occupancy Tax

Hotel occupancy taxes are expected to produce 4.07 percent of Government revenues in 1986–87 on the basis of hotels and guest houses charging their guests 6 percent of the basic accommodation charge.

Passenger Tax

Visitors and residents pay taxes on departure from Bermuda – $10 if departure is by air and $30 if it is by sea. All told, this source is expected to produce 3.39 percent of Government revenues in 1986–87.

Vehicle Licences

Motor vehicle owners in Bermuda must pay annual licence fees which vary according to the size and types of vehicles. Money from this source, it is anticipated, will amount to 3.21 percent of Government revenues in 1986–87.

Stamp Duty

Stamp duty is levied on certain documents at a variety of rates. Duty is payable on an affidavit of value of a deceased's estate at a rate of 2 percent on the first $100,000 and at 5 percent thereafter. The sale or transfer of land incurs duty at one-half percent on the first $100,000 of consideration and at 1 percent beyond that. Stamp duty is also payable on the incorporation of an increase in share capital of companies at one-half percent for local companies and one-quarter percent for international companies. Such duties are expected to yield 2.69 percent of 1986–87 Government revenues.

Other Taxes

There are a variety of other taxes which produce relatively small percentages of total revenue. For example, persons classified as resident for exchange control purposes are liable to a 10 percent overseas investment tax on the purchase of foreign currency used to make investments abroad, or in repaying borrowing undertaken to finance overseas investments. Re-invested dividends are not subject to the tax. As well, current account payments overseas, except interest on foreign borrowing to finance overseas investment, are exempt. Also, non-Bermudians who buy dwellings locally are liable to a 10 percent tax on the purchase price, and there is a 20 percent tax levied on betting stakes.

The USA-Bermuda Tax Convention

On 11 July 1986, the United Kingdom Government, acting on behalf of Bermuda in a matter of international affairs, signed in Washington, D.C. a Convention concerning the taxation of insurance enterprises and mutual assistance in tax matters. The Convention sets up new arrangements between Bermuda and the United States of America in those respects. As part of the package of reciprocal rights and obligations agreed upon, Bermuda has undertaken to facilitate the supply from Bermuda to the United States fiscal authorities of information that may be found in Bermuda relating to tax fraud, tax evasion, and other tax-related matters of concern to the United States. The Bill is a consequence of that undertaking and seeks: (a) to modify Bermudian law by removing impediments to the above-mentioned facilitation; and, (b) to introduce specific procedures for use by the Minister of Finance in obtaining and handling information required by the United States authorities. If this Bill is ratified in the US it will be an important one for both countries. For Bermuda it helps to demonstrate that the country is strictly only interested in legal international business and it may help to discourage any international tax law changes which could conceivably harm Bermuda's international enterprises.

TOURISM

Tourism is not simply a twentieth-century phenomenon for it can be traced back to *Old Testament* records. However, in the mid to late 1900s, tourism has been one of the fastest growing industries in the world. In the latter period, more than 75 percent of the world's tourists originated in the USA and Western Europe – and of that percentage, more than 40 percent were from the USA and West Germany. By far the most popular destination for tourists has been Europe, but North America, Latin America, and the Caribbean are favoured areas.

A UN Conference on Travel and Tourism held in Rome in 1963 defined a 'visitor' as 'any person visiting a country other than that in which he has his usual place of residence, for any reason other than following an occupation remunerated within that country.' Within that definition are 'tourists' who are 'temporary visitors staying at least twenty-four hours for (a) leisure (recreation, holidays, health, study, religion, sport), or (b) business (family, friends, meetings, missions).' On the other hand, 'excursionists' are 'temporary visitors who stay less than twenty-four hours.' Though not universally accepted, the UN excursionist definition does not include cruise passengers and, thus, some countries' arrival statistics often do not measure the real size of a market. And, it is often difficult to determine which categories are included in statistics. However, it is generally agreed that the potential benefits of tourism include: contributions to balance of payments, dispersion of development, contributions to general economic development, the generation of employment, and social benefits. Below, the extent to which these general factors apply in Bermuda is discussed.

Tourism in Bermuda now represents a culminating, almost all encompassing, focus of the islands' history, and it is an economic development of its geological and geographical resources. Hamilton's first hotel opened in 1863 but it was not until the 1880s that Bermuda's reputation as a refuge from the North American winter became more established. One such historic visitor in 1883 was the Marchioness of Lorne, Princess Louise, daughter of Queen Victoria. At the time her husband was the Governor General of Canada and it was Canada's winter from which she sought relief in Bermuda. Apparently she made such an impression on the then sleepy colony that Harley Trott felt there could only be one name for his new hotel – The Princess Hotel, which is still a major resort hotel on Hamilton's waterfront. Incidentally, one of its most loyal guests was Samuel Clemens (Mark Twain) who became a familiar figure to Bermudians as he sat in his rocking chair on the verandah.

Steamships transported the early tourists to Bermuda until they were supplanted by jet aircraft. Of course cruise ships now carry thousands of tourists to Bermuda as is recorded below. The growth of tourism in Bermuda can be seen by glancing at tourist arrival data:

1908	**1913**	**1918**	**1920**	**1926**	**1931**
5,418	21,595	1,345	12,000	27,214	47,376
1938	**1946**	**1956**	**1963**	**1968**	**1974**
52,725	26,000	109,746	105,081	331,379	531,568
1981	**1982**	**1983**	**1984**	**1985**	
535,246	540,805	567,700	528,800	548,700	

It was anticipated that the growth would reflect the US economy's growth in 1984 but, instead, regular arrivals fell by 6.6 percent to 417,461 while the numbers of cruise passengers declined by 7.8 percent to 111,410. Not only were numbers down, but the average length of stay also declined from 5 nights in 1983 to 4.9 nights in 1984. As a result, average occupancy in the hotels fell to 60 percent compared with 63.9 percent in 1983 and 73.9 percent in the peak year of 1980. The strength of the US dollar, which made Europe in particular such an attractive holiday destination in 1984, was perhaps the single most important cause of Bermuda's disappointing season. Local prices, however, were high even before the appreciation of the dollar worsened Bermuda's competitiveness. And, although high prices need not be a critical factor where Bermuda's comparatively small market is concerned, clearly the price differential compared with other destinations, and exacerbated by extremely high air fares, was sufficiently large in 1984 to depress the number of visitors.

Expectations were that 1985 would be one of mixed fortunes because the Castle Harbour Hotel (now Marriott's) would be closed the entire season so that extensive renovations could be carried out, and Village Hotel of Bermuda (Club Med and formerly Loew's Beach Hotel) would be closed part of the season for the same reason. However, it was expected that the number of cruise passengers would increase. In fact, the number of regular arrivals was down by 11,600 (2.8 percent) to 405,861, but hotel occupancy rose to 65 percent and the average length of stay remained at 4.9 nights. As was forecast, the number of cruise passengers did increase by 31,429 (28 percent) to 142,839. Cruise passengers, because their accommodation is found on board ships and their average stay is much less than regular visitors, do not contribute as much to the economy. They are, nevertheless, an important part of the tourism economy for they spend about $25 per head per day in shops compared with regular visitors' spending of $20. In 1985, they accounted for an estimated $10 million of retail sales out of a tourist total of almost $50 million. Overall in 1985, the 548,700 tourists had 8,918 beds available to them and it was provisionally estimated that they spent $357 million.

Data on 1986 tourism are not yet available but there is reason for optimism. First, the decline in the dollar improves Bermuda's competitiveness against Europe, Mexico, and some Caribbean countries which enjoyed a substantial increase in American visitors in recent years. Also, Europe's tourism declined in 1986 because of terrorist threats. Second, the opening of Club Med in March 1986, and the Marriott-

Castle Harbour in April 1986, with the prospect of good occupancies in both establishments, should have boosted the total number of regular arrivals. Third, the Department of Tourism had lined up another excellent cruise programme, with arrivals spread more widely through the week and with a ship calling regularly at St. George's.

In 1973, 86.8 percent of Bermuda's tourists came from the USA, 7.8 percent from Canada, 3 percent from the UK, 1.3 percent from Europe, and 1.1 percent from other countries. Over the most recent three years for which data are available, the situation has changed little but shows even more reliance on the US market. In 1985, 89.2 percent of tourists originated in the USA, 6.3 percent in Canada, 2.5 percent in the UK, 0.9 percent in Europe, and 1.1 percent from other countries. Generally, about one quarter of US visitors are from New York State while most of the remainder originate in Massachusetts, New Jersey, Connecticut, Pennsylvania, and Rhode Island. Most Canadian visitors are from Ontario, Quebec, and the Atlantic Provinces. These figures clearly indicate where the market must be consolidated but also show where there may be opportunities for new thrusts – particularly in the off-season.

The following shows the visitors' arrivals by month in 1984 (numbers include cruise passengers but they are shown separately in brackets): January 9,536 (683), February 15,362 (456), March 33,955 (none), April 51,021 (8,902), May 68,064 (15,818), June 61,370 (13,776), July 62,484 (20,115), August 66,966 (21,076), September 60,048 (17,919), October 53,976 (12,665), November 30,322 (none), December 15,767 (none).

Generally, about 30 percent of Bermuda's visitors are in the 20–29 age range and this is probably largely because of US college weeks and honeymooners. Approximately 50 percent are over forty years of age with about 10 percent being over sixty. Most visitors have incomes in mid to upper ranges.

Small islands are known generally to have problems associated with tourism development. It is often the case that foreign control, or dominance, develops which in turn leads to high leakage from the local island economy and there is a consequent low economic multiplier effect. To illustrate this point, it is clear that international airlines transport tourists to small islands and hotels are often owned by foreigners. Similarly is the case with cruise liners. Also, generally, it is not uncommon for tourism in small islands to become almost monopoly industries at the potential expense of other possibilities. If this occurs there is likely to be seasonal unemployment, and that obviously has the potential to lead to there being political and social tensions. The latter dysfunctional consequences can also occur when local, relatively poor island residents come into contact with seemingly free-spending high-living tourists who appear wealthy (even though they may not be wealthy but rather they are spending a year's vacation savings). Another potential problem in small island tourism economies is that of saturation – that is, too many tourists for the local attractive tourist resources. So, to what extent do these potential problems manifest themselves in Bermuda?

First an attempt will be made to try to illustrate what a dollar spent in Bermuda is really worth to the Bermudian economy. Such estimations must be viewed with caution but they are probably 'in the right order' as Young stated after making the attempt in 1974 – he used a method similar to the following current example. First an estimate is made of what would happen to a first round daily expenditure in Bermuda of a tourist $100. It may look something like:

	Original expense by tourist per day ($)	Less foreign expense	First Round Bermudian Income
Room	30	2	28
Food	36	18	18
Entertainment	16.5	3	13.5
Merchandise	17.5	7	10.5
Total	100	30	70

Thus 70 percent is then available for circulation in the Bermudian economy. Subsequent rounds of expenditure would be along the following lines:

(1) In every expenditure 81 percent ends up in the hands of an

individual in Bermuda available for spending or saving.
(2) Of personal disposable income 77 percent ends up as personal consumption expenses.
(3) Of personal consumption expenditure 70 percent is spent on imported goods and services while the balance represents expenditure on Bermudian goods and services.
(4) Combining these factors it is seen that second round spending generated in Bermuda by a \$1 of expenditure of average character is about \$0.20 (\$1.00 × 0.81 × 0.77 × 0.30). This means that 80 percent of the first round expenditure represents leakage to imports, savings, retained earnings by businesses, personal taxes, etc.
(5) To determine the multiplier to apply to first round income the following addition is necessary:

\$1.00	(First round)
0.20	(Second round)
0.04	(Third round; 0.2 × 0.2)
0.008	(Fourth round; 0.2 × 0.2 × 0.2)
1.25	(Rounded)

This general multiplier is that used to calculate the full contribution of tourism to Bermuda's economy.

(6) Total tourism expenditures (1985)	\$357 million
Less foreign purchases (30 percent)	\$107 million
Equals first round income	\$250 million

Total contribution to economy is \$250m × 1.25 = \$312.5m

Thus by dividing the total contribution of tourism (\$312.5m) by the total tourist expenditure (\$357m) a multiplier of 0.87 is obtained. So, every dollar spent in Bermuda by a tourist provides 87 cents in real income to Bermuda. It is perhaps worth reiterating that this is an estimate but one which is probably in the right order.

There is an optimum number of tourists an area can entertain and, above which, the costs of tourism outweigh the advantages – that is, saturation is reached. This situation is theoretically explicit but it is practically elusive in Bermuda. Initial factors involve available labour, and land for hotels, roads, and tourist attractions. Excesses lead to difficulties. For example, land used for tourists means less land is available for housing, schools, and open spaces. Excessive emphasis on tourism leads to seasonal unemployment and so threatens the economic structure. Excessive tourism puts pressures on the urban infrastructure – particularly on transport. The combination of these negative factors can easily alienate the local population. Issues of land, housing, and jobs are dealt with elsewhere in this book but here, it is perhaps sufficient to state that hostility to tourists is very rare in Bermuda. Perhaps this is because the economic gulf between hosts and visitors in Bermuda is not so great as in the Caribbean. There is perhaps some hostility between the Bermudian workforce and the non-Bermudian workforce but, as stated elsewhere, a Bermudianisation policy is in place. Finally, here, if the land of Bermuda had to be used to support its own population, it is estimated that the population could only be 5,000. Consequently, it is not an option to reject tourism as the major industry of Bermuda.

And, for Bermuda to continue to prosper economically from tourism the industry will have to pay close attention to its costs and prices in recognition of the fact that tourism is an intensely competitive industry, in which future growth will occur only in those areas that offer the best value for money. As the Minister of Finance said in his 1986–87 Budget Statement, 'The coming year will provide us with a tremendous opportunity to publicise Bermuda through our visitors. This can best be done by all of us extending to our visitors the warmth and friendliness which has traditionally been our hallmark, and which is potentially the best advertisement of all for Bermuda.'

INTERNATIONAL BUSINESS

The various taxes received by the Government from international companies were described earlier in this chapter but here the more general aspects of such enterprises are discussed. Broadly, the companies involved are likely to be ones with world-wide sources of income that seek to consolidate their international income in one centre so as to avoid, legitimately, the heavy taxation to which they would be subject in many countries. The companies are 'exempted' or 'non-resident' (also called permit or overseas companies), but both types can only carry out their main business outside of Bermuda. The exempted companies are constituted in Bermuda and are exempted from requirements of registering the nationality or occupation of any of their shareholders or the amount paid for shares or share transfers. In particular, they are exempt from those aspects of Bermuda law that restrict the portion of capital which may be held by non-Bermudians. Under existing legislation, local Bermuda companies (for trade and operations within Bermuda) must be at least 60 percent owned and controlled by Bermudians. As well, they may obtain exemption from possible future income tax, profit or capital gains tax over a period up to 2006. If the previously mentioned USA–Bermuda Tax Convention is ratified some modification may be made but the general principles will remain the same. The non-resident businesses are incorporated abroad and acquire restricted residential status in Bermuda. Except for a special group of insurance companies, they are not permitted to engage in any trade or business in the islands unless by special permit with time limitations and conditions.

Today, international business is Bermuda's second industry and it includes companies dealing with insurance, oil, computer software licensing, investment holding and finance, shipping, and communications as well as local professional firms that serve the industry in such areas as law, accounting, banking, and insurance. Between 1935, when international businesses began operating in Bermuda, and 1970 the number of companies grew to 2,000. A major impetus was given by the 1950 Exempt Companies' Act which was a calculated bid to attract international companies to the islands by lifting the restrictions prohibiting non-Bermudians from doing business from bases in Bermuda.

Since 1970, the number of international companies has continued to grow though at a reduced rate in recent years. Recent development occurred as follows:

1980	1981	1982	1983	1984
5,088	5,422	5,565	5,781	5,861

The 1984 total of 5,861 international exempted and non-resident companies on the register was an increase of 1.4 percent over the previous year. However, during 1984, a number of companies, principally in the insurance sector, announced cutbacks in their local operations. Then, in 1984–85 international company expenditure in Bermuda was flat and has shown no real growth since 1980–81. But, since the main component of international companies' spending is on wages and salaries, it is not surprising that employment within the sector has followed a similar pattern. It reached a peak of 2,314 jobs in 1982, but fell each year for three years to 1,973 in 1985. The Minister of Finance is keen to generate more international business and to counter the trend. To that end in his 1986–87 budget, he reduced stamp duties on exempted insurance companies, mutual funds, and personal trusts where the settlement involves property situated outside Bermuda. He also plans to step up Government's involvement in the promotion of international business, recognising that its contribution to the economy on some measures is not far short of tourism's. Those interested in the detailed regulations concerning international business are advised to consult the Exempted Undertakings Tax Protection Act of 1966 and the Companies Act, 1981 and 1982, which defines certain restrictions regarding the otherwise liberal activities of exempt companies.

At the time of the 1986–87 Budget Statement, the Minister feared that the tax reform legislation under discussion in Washington could lead to the federal excise tax on re-insurance premiums rising from 1 percent to 4 percent. If enacted, it would materially damage the financial viability of many of the exempted reinsurance companies operating in Bermuda. This is an indication of how little ultimate control Bermuda can exert over international business and, therefore, how absolutely important it is to take great care with any endeavours associated with tourism.

Banking

Banking services in Bermuda cover a wide range of personal and business financial transactions, beginning with basic chequing and savings accounts, to loans, cash management, international payments, and foreign exchange. The high calibre of such services was critical in first attracting international businesses to Bermuda. The islands' banks have capabilities in all areas of service, enhanced by international affiliations and extensive up-to-date telecommunications and data-communications systems. Close relationships are maintained with leading brokerage and banking firms of the world thus enabling immediate trading of securities anywhere in the world on behalf of personal or corporate clients.

Professional support services have also flourished as the international business community has expanded. There are many excellent law firms in Bermuda and, similarly, major worldwide accounting firms are represented in Bermuda which provide a complete range of services. Bermuda's three banks are the Bermuda Commercial Bank, the Bank of Bermuda, and the Bank of N. T. Butterfield and Son. All three banks can give financial information to those interested and they have correspondent banks and representatives in New York, London, Canada, and Hong Kong.

There are no restrictions on the import into Bermuda of bank notes expressed in any currency. Visitors are allowed to take with them on departure any foreign currency notes which they brought with them. It should be noted that it is illegal for foreign currency to be bought or sold in Bermuda other than from or to an authorised dealer, that is one of the three banks. This restriction does not, however, prevent foreign currency notes being tendered for purchases of goods and services in Bermuda if acceptable to the vendor.

OVERALL ECONOMIC OPPORTUNITIES

The Bermuda Labour Department's surveys of jobs filled are useful for monitoring employment and economic activity trends. When incorporated with the Bermuda Standard Classification of Occupations (BSCO) the combined data are helpful to career and guidance counsellors and students in identifying the kinds of occupations in Bermuda and the extent to which they exist. Also, the BSCO indicates the general nature of education, training, and personnel requirements demanded in each occupation. The following figures show the growth in the number of filled jobs in Bermuda in recent years:

	1979	**1980**	**1983**	**1984**	**1985**
Jobs	28,832	29,669	31,812	32,033	32,190

Since 1983, approximately 80 percent of the jobs filled were held by Bermudians and 20 percent by non-Bermudians. In the same period, women have held just over 45 percent of the jobs. In 1985, the hours worked per week for each worker averaged 34.5 while the average employment income was $21,700 in the 1983–84 fiscal year (the most recent for which published data are available).

The survey shows that, in 1985, the following numbers of jobs were filled in the various categories listed here: agriculture, fishing, and quarrying (339); manufacturing (1,172); electricity, gas, and water (425); construction (2,378); wholesale and retail (5,162); hotels and restaurants (5,835); transport and communications (2,176); banks, insurance, and business services (4,386); public administration (3,983); community and personal services (3,565); international companies (1,973); and, other (796).

Although employment patterns do not tend to vary much from year to year, it is possible to discern changes over a longer period. Since 1980, the largest gains in employment have been recorded in finance and insurance (570) and in construction (410). The shares of total employment accounted for by these two sectors have risen from 5.9 percent to 7.3 percent, and from 6 percent to 6.9 percent respectively. Over the same period, the biggest fall (142) has occurred in the hotels and restaurants, which have seen their share of total employment decline from 21 percent in 1980, a peak year for tourism, to 19 percent in 1984. The international company sector has had mixed fortunes, with its share of total employment initially rising from 6.2 percent in 1980 to 7.3

percent in 1982, before falling back to 6.4 percent by the end of 1984.

Professor Ted Gurr's 1984 'Quality of Life' report demonstrates that Bermudians have a remarkably high level of satisfaction with their jobs. Overall, 86 percent of the people surveyed said they were satisfied with their jobs – this compares with a similar US figure of 80 percent. The high level of satisfaction in Bermuda is evident for virtually all demographic groups. 75 percent of employed black youths are satisfied, 88 percent of white youths, and these proportions increase among older groups, so that over 90 percent of adults over forty, black and white, are satisfied. There are only slight differences between women and men – 88 percent of men and 84 percent of women are satisfied. Also, even in the lowest family-income category, 82 percent are satisfied with their jobs.

Bermudians also think they they have fair chances for job advancement. More than two-thirds of both whites and blacks share this optimism while the most dissatisfied group is that of younger adults aged twenty-one to thirty, of whom more than one-third are not satisfied with prospects for job advancement. It seems this is brought on by too few senior positions.

The majority of Bermudians in all demographic and income groups agree with the proposition that the available jobs are interesting and fulfilling, and that Bermuda is an open society. Contrary to these views, two-thirds of all Bermudians, including whites and blacks, prosperous and poor, believe that some people have more economic opportunities and advantages than others. In Gurr's survey people were not asked which people nor what advantages, but their scepticism may be linked to the widespread concern that foreigners are taking jobs that they think rightfully should go to Bermudians. This can be interpreted as widespread support for the Government's Bermudianisation policies.

Of different economic concern is the belief of 55 percent of people surveyed that men are paid more than women for the same type of work. Whites and blacks, men and women, all agree in similar percentages though there is no comprehensive objective evidence at present.

AGRICULTURE AND FISHERIES

In the past, agriculture was a mainstay of Bermuda's economy but the increase in population and buildings has greatly decreased the land available for such activity. A glance at the amount of arable land available in this century illustrates the point.

	1921	**1931**	**1941**	**1951**	**1961**	**1985**
Hectares	1218.9	844.6	607.0	408.3	323.7	244.0
Acres	3012	2087	1500	1009	800	603

Of course it is not simply the increased number of people and buildings which caused this decrease in available arable land, for economic forces were at work. Young showed how the net return from 0.4 ha (1 acre) of potatoes expressed as a percentage of the land value decreased dramatically over about a thirty-year period. The table illustrates:

Year	Net Return ($)	Land Value per 0.4 ha (1 acre) ($)	% Return
1939	225	1,500	15
1958	474	9,000	5.3
1971	541	30,000	1.8

However, despite this decline, tourists like to see some agricultural and horticultural activity when they escape from their pressures at home. And, the production of local food is an important aspect of the economy in that it provides jobs, saves on international exchange, and is the only totally secure source of food. Thus, the table below demonstrates how arable land is currently (1985 data) used and the dollar value of local food production.

	ha	(acres)	($000)
Vegetable production	140	(347)	3,700
Fruit production	36	(90)	900
Flower production	3	(8)	
Pasture	19	(48)	
Forage	12	(30)	

	ha	(acres)	($000)
Fallow	32	(80)	
Milk			1,053
Eggs			800
Meat			400
Honey			175
Total	244	(603)	7,098

The total production is only a small percentage of the overall food consumption. Egg production covers about 50 percent of the total requirements; milk about 20 percent; potatoes 56 percent, other vegetables 50 percent; and, citrus fruit and bananas 50 percent. It should be noted that vegetable production is the most important branch of agriculture.

Within the above agricultural production, Bermuda has been well known abroad for its onions, citrus fruit, bananas, and the Easter lily. The latter was particularly famous and, in 1945, there were 20.2 ha (50 acres) planted in lilies which were a great attraction for Easter tourists. As well, 4,000 cases of bulbs were exported to US and UK markets. However, by 1960 the planted area had fallen to 4.8 ha (12 acres). Prior to the high US tariff on vegetables, onions were popular exports to the extent that Hamilton was called 'Onion Town'. However, US growers discovered how to simulate Bermuda's growing conditions, then cornered the seed market, and finally registered the name as 'Bermuda Onions'. However, the onion has left its mark since Bermudians are often referred to as 'Onions', and the biennial Bermuda ocean yacht race from Newport, R.I., is popularly termed 'the thrash to the Onion Patch.'

The bucolic ambience necessary for tourism, quite apart from that provided by working farmers, is cultivated by the Government's Department of Agriculture and Fisheries. The Department is responsible for the impeccably manicured hedges along the 125 miles of the islands' public roads, the beautifully landscaped parks and roundabouts, the Agricultural Exhibition, the Botanical Gardens, and the clean public beaches. Additionally, the Department provides a variety of services designed to enhance Bermuda's agricultural industry. Services include testing cattle for tuberculosis, vaccinating cattle to prevent brucellosis, inspecting large imported animals, controlling plant pests and diseases by spraying, and carrying out research programmes. Finally, to assist farmers, the Government operates a wholesale marketing centre for the purchase and resale of local produce. With agriculture practised in small holdings, many farmers sell directly to their consumers though they often also avail themselves of the marketing centre's services.

Fisheries

Bermuda's reefs are sources of food and shelter for most of the fish and shellfish caught by the islands' commercial and recreational fishermen. Traditionally, the industry has centred on reef-dwelling species of fish such as grouper, snappers, porgy, and spiny lobsters, with jack and tuna playing a secondary role. However, during the past decade, the catches of these traditionally important species have shown drastic declines. As a result, fishermen have been making better use of formerly under-utilised species such as tuna, wahoo, parrot fish, surgeon fish, amberjack, shark, and chub which are taken from the main island platform and the Challenger and Argus banks.

Currently, the objectives of the fisheries programme are to support and develop the local fishing industry in order to exploit and harvest all resources efficiently to their maximum sustainable levels. Emphasis is placed on fisheries' conservation and in providing the professional and technical services necessary for this purpose. Essentially, the programme involves fisheries' conservation, research, the licensing and regulation of fishermen, and the operation of a small processing and marketing facility.

Bermuda has about 275 registered fishermen operating some 210 licensed fishing vessels. The use of fish pots is estimated to account for approximately 59 percent of the total catch of fish and for all lobsters. Some 135 vessels are licensed to use pots.

Most of the catch, about 75 percent, is distributed to hotels and restaurants. A pilot fish processing and marketing plant,

Sargasso Seafoods, was established in 1980 by the Government with United Nations' assistance to improve the marketing of formerly under-utilised species. However, most fishermen traditionally process and sell their own catches.

DOMESTIC DEMAND

Domestic economic demand in Bermuda is manifested in consumers' expenditure, Government consumption, and capital formation.

In 1984–85, average earnings rose 8 percent while inflation averaged 5 percent. Consumer spending as a result rose by 3 percent in real terms. In the most recent year for which there are records – 1985–86 – earnings continued to outpace inflation, rising by some 6 percent to 7 percent, while inflation fell to an annual rate of about 3.5 percent. However, in that year, consumer credit was less readily available because of the banks' tightened lending criteria, and so growth in overall consumer spending is likely to have been shown to be subdued when final data are in.

The retail sales' figures also suggest that 1985 was not a strong year for spending. Retail sales, which form about half of consumer spending, were down 2 percent in value in 1985. Since prices rose by 3.5 percent, the drop in the dollar value of sales implies a significant reduction in the volume of business. Part of the fall may have been due to the reduced number of regular visitors. Tighter credit conditions, however, are likely to have been the most important factor in depressing sales. There was, for example, a sharp drop in sales of motor vehicles after two previously good years. In millions of dollars this is how consumers spent their money in 1984–85: food, beverages, and tobacco 130.5; housing, light, and power 183.4; clothing and footwear 40.7; household goods and services 100.3; and, other goods and services 264.0.

The Minister of Finance expected to see a modest rise in consumer spending in 1986. Pay settlements continued to outstrip inflation, and there was no drop in employment, so that employment income appeared set to continue to rise in real terms. With the expected upturn in tourism injecting additional money into the economy, and with banks continuing to lend for consumer purchases, consumer spending was expected to grow by 2 percent in 1986–87.

Government current spending rose by 3 percent in real terms in 1984–85 and a similar rise was estimated for 1985–86. The growth reflects increased provision of services for tourism, the police, the judiciary, the prison service, and on increased subsidies for public transport.

In 1984–85, gross fixed capital formation rose by 15 percent in real terms, with substantial gains recorded in housing, and in investment in plant and machinery (particularly in the power-generating and telecommunications sectors). The rate of housebuilding remained high and there was substantial investment in renovations and improvements at some major hotels. As a result, the construction industry has remained buoyant. The major capital outlays by hotels were a welcome indication to the Government of the hotels' long-term confidence in the future of Bermuda. The Finance Minister believed that, once all the projects were completed – at Marriott's, Club Med, the Princess Hotels, and others – the physical plant of the tourist industry would surpass that which could be found in any other resort destination. Certainly, the amenities are very fine.

OVERALL ECONOMIC SUMMARIES

The most recent Bermuda Monetary Authority published summary data on the islands' economic status are quite positive and illustrate why the Minister of Finance is cautiously optimistic. The figures are recorded in the following short tables.

Bermuda Gross Domestic Product at Constant Prices (1975/76 BD $ Millions)

	1983–84
Consumers' expenditure	339.5
General Government final consumption	53.6
Gross domestic fixed capital formation	89.7
Domestic demand	482.8
Exports: Visitor expenditure	151.9
Exports: International Company expenditures	88.0
Exports: Other goods and services	59.9
External demand	299.8
Total Final Demand	782.6
Less: Imports of Goods and services	−318.9
Gross domestic product at market prices	463.7

1984 Balance of Payments Estimates ($ million)

Visible trade balance	−366
Shipment account balance	− 50
Other transportation balance	− 1
Travel account balance	+273
Investment income balance	+ 27
Mgt., prof., & tech. services balance	+205
Other goods, services and income balance	− 72
Unrequited transfer	− 37
Current Account	− 21
Total Capital Account	+ 27
Errors and omissions	− 6

Note: +indicates inflow
−indicates outflow

6 VACATION ISLAND

Mark Twain is also supposed to have said that, 'Bermuda is paradise but one has to go through hell to get there.' Fortunately, this is no longer the case from a transit perspective, but it is still 'paradise' in that its basic attractions remain the same – a warm and gentle climate, cleanliness, outstanding scenic beauty, vivid colours, fragrant scents, and a friendly atmosphere. Bermuda is remote, secluded, cosy, and separate from many of life's frantic pressures. Visitors find cricket, high tea, pubs, bobbies, and left-hand driving but it's not Britain. Guests wander leisurely, they settle in over-stuffed easy chairs, sip cocktails on a terrace, linger by a pool, jog on a beach, play tennis, dine elegantly or simply, see a show, and retire early or dance the night away. Overall, Bermuda has a 40 percent return rate among its visitors, and many people return year after year.

This chapter contains: some particulars a first-time visitor to Bermuda may want to know before embarking, advice on getting there, where to stay on arrival, how to travel around, what to see, what to do, where to shop, and where to go after dark.

PREPARATIONS

The Bermuda Department of Tourism (BDT) has responsibility for such concerns as advertising, public relations, social events, and overseas communications. It produces excellent timely supplies of brochures and maps which cover trip planning, accommodation, sports, and a host of other pertinent material. So, one way to start gathering information is to contact the nearest Bermuda Department of Tourism

Office. Their locations are:
(1) Global House, 43 Church Street, Hamilton 5-24, Bermuda.
(2) Suite 201, 310 Madison Avenue, New York, N.Y. 10017.
(3) Suite 1070, Randolph-Wacker Building, 150N Wacker Drive, Chicago, Illinois 60606.
(4) Suite 2008, 235 Peachtree Street, NE, Atlanta, Georgia 30303.
(5) Suite 1010, 44 School Street, Boston, Massachusetts, 02108.
(6) Western Region Representative, J.A. Tetley, Inc., Suite 601, 3075 Wilshire Boulevard, Los Angeles, CA 90010.
(7) European Representative, Bermuda Tourism, BCB Ltd., 6 Burnsall Street, London, SW3 3ST.

Alternatively, local travel agents often can serve prospective visitors well because the BDT supplies them with ample information and has a programme to invite about 1,000 travel agents per year to visit the islands and so keep abreast of developments in facilities, rates, and booking trends. Agents know about the BDT's 'Space Service' and they should be able to find out which wholesale tour operators have Bermuda packages for sale via retail travel agents.

Costs

Early enquiries are certainly worthwhile from a financial perspective so that the best deals can be sought. Because Bermuda is a high quality resort country, its prices have to be quite high. A typical day for one person at a luxury hotel is likely to cost about $150 while the cost when staying at a more modest hotel would be approximately $125. However, those who intend to spend less on their vacations can easily do so by staying in housekeeping cottages or guest houses. Thus, there are ample opportunities for people of very varied means – and the natural beauty is free!

When To Go

In deciding when to go to Bermuda it is useful to note the climatic features recorded in the first chapter. The change of season comes during mid-November to mid-December and from late March through April. This means that summer weather occurs from late March/April until mid-November/December and then spring-like weather prevails during the remainder of the year. Thus, Bermuda is a year-round resort with no rainy season and a climate which does not interfere with the enjoyment of outdoor activities. So, with these points in mind, anytime in the year is quite appropriate for a visit though it can be cheaper when the demand is less (see Chapter 5).

Getting There

It is always necessary to check the current travel situation with an agent or carrier. However, to illustrate the likely range of possibilities, the late 1986 arrangements are recorded here:

(By Air)

From the USA: American Airlines direct from La Guardia (New York) and Boston; Delta Airlines direct from Hartford, Boston, and Atlanta; Eastern Airlines from New York, Newark, Philadelphia, Baltimore, and Atlanta; Pan Am direct from New York; British Airways direct from Baltimore and Orlando.

From Canada: Air Canada direct from Toronto and Halifax (and with exceptionally favourable terms for Western Canadians who are travelling to Toronto).

From the UK: British Airways from London.

From other countries: British Airways have direct and connecting flights from the Bahamas, West Indies, and South America.

(By Ship)

From the USA: Weekly services: Home Lines *Atlantic* and *Homeric* from New York (April to October); Bahama Cruise Line *Bermuda Star* from New York (May to October); Royal Caribbean Cruise Line *Nordic Prince* (May to September). Other weekly schedules with one- or two-day stops in Bermuda include Chandris Lines

Americanis and *Galileo* from New York (May to October). Periodic sailings of other cruise ships leaving US ports are available.

From the UK: Cruise ships of the P&O Line en route between Australia, New Zealand, and the UK call in Bermuda.

Most likely Mark Twain would agree that it can now be paradise getting there. One recent batch of US cruise passengers, who were too jaded to even leave the ship at some Caribbean islands, were captivated by Bermuda – particularly the cleanliness of the streets, the pastel homes, the handsome churches, the pretty shops, and the bobbies in their Bermuda shorts and helmets. So much so they kept running out of film as they snapped coves, yachts, flowers, lighthouses, forts, houses, and people.

Travel Documents

A return or onward ticket or other document of onward transportation to a country which, at that time the passenger has right of entry, is required by all visitors. Visas are not required except for Iron Curtain Nationals and nationals of Argentina, Cuba, Iran, Iraq and Libya. (Note: any of the above nationals who are permanent residents of the US or Canada, holding a valid US Alien Registration Card or valid proof of Canadian Landed Immigrant Status plus a valid passport, do not require a visa to enter Bermuda.) However, persons requiring a visa to enter other countries on departure from Bermuda must be in possession of the respective visa prior to arrival in Bermuda. Passports are required by all visitors from countries which require a passport for re-entry purposes or for entry through another country which at that time they have right-of-entry. (Note: in fact, just about every visitor entering Bermuda requires a passport with the exception of US citizens.)

All travellers must carry with them proof of citizenship and personal identification relevant to return to their own country or for re-entry through another foreign country. Visitors from the United States are required by Bermuda Immigration Authorities to have in their possession any one of the following items: (a) passport, if expired should be of sufficiently recent vintage so that photograph resembles bearer, (b) birth certificate or certified copy, (c) US re-entry permit, (d) US voter's registration card if it shows bearer's signature, (e) US Naturalisation Certificate, (f) US Alien Registration Card. (Note: driver's licence is not acceptable as proof of citizenship.) Visitors from Canada are required by Bermuda Immigration Authorities to have in their possession either a valid passport, a Canadian Certificate of Citizenship, or a valid passport plus proof of their Landed Immigrant Status.

No smallpox vaccination certificates are required from any travellers except those who, within the preceeding fourteen days, have been in a country, any part of which is infected.

All bona fide visitors may remain in Bermuda for a reasonable period of time – permission for long stays may be sought from the Chief Immigration Officer, Ministry of Labour and Home Affairs, PO Box HM 1364, Hamilton 5.

Customs

Visitors may take into Bermuda – duty free – all wearing apparel and articles for their personal use, including sports equipment, cameras, golf bags, etc. Also 50 cigars, 200 cigarettes, .454 kgs (1 lb) tobacco, 1.137 litres (1 qt.) liquor, 1.137 litres (1 qt.) wine. Visitors are permitted to bring in duty free approximately 20 lbs of meat. Other foodstuffs may be dutiable at 5.5–22.5 percent of value. All imports may be inspected upon arrival. Visitors entering Bermuda may claim a $25 duty free gift allowance. Note: clearance of merchandise and sales materials for use by conventions must be arranged for in advance with the hotel concerned.

Importation of, possession of, or dealing with unlawful drugs (including marijuana) is an offence. Anyone contravening this act is liable to fines of up to $5,000 or three years imprisonment or both. Conviction on indictment carries a maximum penalty of a fine or twenty years imprisonment, or both. Customs officers may, at their discretion, conduct body searches for drugs and other uncustomed goods. Similarly, firearms and ammunition may not be imported.

Credit Cards
Mastercard, Visa, American Express, Carte Blanche, and Diners' Club credit cards are accepted at most shops and restaurants throughout Bermuda. However, many hotels and guest houses do not accept credit cards and so it is worth checking – travel agents are informed.

Clothing
The atmosphere of a Bermuda hotel, guest house or cottage colony, and indeed of Bermuda itself, is one of British reserve and dignified informality. Therefore, there are certain 'customs of dress' which are of interest. As a rule of thumb, dress conservatively. Bathing suits, abbreviated tops and short shorts are not acceptable except at beaches and pools. In public (including public areas of hotels) beach wear must be covered. Bare feet and hair curlers are not acceptable anywhere in public. It is an offence to ride cycles or appear in public without a shirt or just wearing a bathing suit top. (Joggers may wear standard running shorts and shirts.) Casual sports wear is acceptable in restaurants at lunch time but most restaurants and night clubs in and out of hotels require gentlemen to wear a jacket and tie in the evenings. It is best to check on dress requirements when making dinner/night club reservations, as some places do have casual evenings periodically. The following list summarises requirements.

Warmer Months: May to mid-November.
Women: summer-weight sport clothes, cotton dresses, swim suits, casuals of lightweight travel fabrics, a light dressy sweater or wrap for evening, cocktail-type outfits for evenings, a raincoat or lightweight wind breaker.
Men: summer-weight sports clothes, swim suits, lightweight suit or sports jacket and tie for evenings, a raincoat or lightweight wind breaker.

Cooler Months: December to late March.
Women: light woollens or autumn-weight casuals, sweaters, skirts, slacks, dressier sweater or wrap and cocktail-type outfits

for evenings, raincoat and warmer jacket, wind breaker or coat, with swim suit for warmer days.

Men: light woollens or autumn-weight casuals, sports jacket, slacks, sweaters, suit or sports jacket and tie for evenings, raincoat and warmer jacket, wind breaker or coat, with swim wear for warmer days.

Change of Seasons: mid-November through December and late March through April. Either spring or summer weather may occur and a combination of the two above suggestions should be ideal.

Formal Dress: not necessary, except for specific personal needs. Tuxedos, morning suits, evening tail may be rented by visitors, but accessories must be purchased.

Electricity

Throughout Bermuda the electricity is 110 volt, 60 cycle alternating current so that appliances taken to the islands from the US and Canada do not need adaptors – those taken there from Europe do.

Marriage in Bermuda

Visitors who wish to marry while in Bermuda must have their 'Notice of Intended Marriage' published in the Bermuda newspapers. Only those normally resident in the UK who intend to marry a British subject resident in Bermuda may have their banns called in church instead. 'Notice of Intended Marriage' application forms may be obtained from BTA offices and must then be submitted with a fee of $75 to the Registrar General, Government Administration Building, Parliament Street, Hamilton 5–24. Such planning should be started early and checks need to be made about the particular churches' requirements.

Disabled Visitors

Bermuda is a branch location of the Society for the Advancement of Travel for the Handicapped (SATH) and the Society will advise on all aspects of travel to, and in, Bermuda for disabled people. For detailed information, write to SATH, PO

Box HM449, Hamilton 5. Tel: (809-29) 5-2525. Generally, it is advisable to make requirements known to hotels, cottage colonies, or guest houses ahead of arrival so that suitable accommodation can be planned.

Hay Fever
The Bermuda climate is relatively favourable for hay fever sufferers. There is no rag-weed and pollens of other weeds are quickly blown out to sea.

ACCOMMODATION

In 1969, the Bermuda Hotels (Licensing and Control) Act and accompanying regulations were passed by the Legislature and provided for the annual inspection and licensing of every property taking six or more paying guests at any one time. As well, at about the same time, the Government instituted a hotel phasing policy with a view to limiting the provision of new hotel beds in proportion to the annual increase of visitor arrivals, and also to take into account visitor amenities and the labour force. With such safeguards in place, Bermuda has, according to the discerning *Penguin Travel Guides*, '. . . more attractive guest rooms per square mile than any other resort island in the world.' The accommodation is divided into the following seven classifications:

1. Large Hotels (Resort type)
2. Small Hotels
3. Cottage Colonies
4. Clubs (Private)
5. Housekeeping Cottages and Apartments (Large and small)
6. Guest Houses (Large and small)
7. Small Properties (Five rooms or fewer).

In most establishments check-in time is 3:00 pm, check-out time is noon, and the following meal plans are operable:
MAP – Modified American Plan (room, breakfast and dinner)
BP – Bermuda Plan (room and breakfast)
CP – Continental Plan (room and light breakfast)
EP – European Plan (room only)
AP – American Plan (room, breakfast, lunch and dinner).

It is usually advisable to work through a travel agent or, better still, a trusted friend when selecting accommodation. However, this section provides some detail of what is available.

Large Hotels (Resort Type)
Most offer a choice of MAP, BP, or EP. A few offer MAP or just EP.

The Belmont Hotel, Golf and Beach Club
P.O. Box WK 251,
Warwick 7, Bermuda
Tel: 809-296-1301

The Bermudiana Hotel
P.O. Box HM 842,
Hamilton 5, Bermuda
Tel: 809-295-1211

Club Med, St George's Cove Village
P.O. Box GE 59,
St. George's 1, Bermuda
Tel: 809-297-8222

Elbow Beach Hotel
P.O. Box HM 455,
Hamilton 5, Bermuda
Tel: 809-296-3535

Grotto Bay Beach Hotel and Tennis Club
P.O. Box HM 1291,
Hamilton 5, Bermuda
Tel: 809-293-8333

Inverurie Hotel
P.O. Box HM 1189,
Hamilton 5, Bermuda
Tel: 809-296-1000

Marriott's Castle Harbour Resort
Tuckers Town,
Hamilton Parish 2-02,
Bermuda
Tel: 809-293-8161
New York Sales Office
(212) 603-8200 or (800) 223-6388

The Princess
P.O. Box HM 837,
Hamilton 5, Bermuda
Tel: 809-295-3000

Sonesta Beach Hotel
P.O. Box HM 1070,
Hamilton 5, Bermuda
Tel: 809-298-8122

Southampton Princess
P.O. Box HM 1379,
Hamilton 5, Bermuda
Tel: 809-296-8000

(*opposite*) Golf courses and outdoor recreations. Bermuda offers year-round opportunities for a wide range of outdoor recreations. It has more golf courses per square mile than any island on earth

12
12
15
15

(*above and top right*) Sailing and water sports are possible in ideal conditions. The right-hand picture shows Flatts Village with the Bermuda Aquarium on the right

Shopping is enjoyable in Bermuda and visitors are usually delighted to find international goods such as European sweaters, bone china, crystal, and perfumes. This is one of many shops at Somers Wharf in St. George's

One of the many stores on Front Street in Hamilton

Small Hotels
Generally MAP is offered but other meal plans are available.

Glencoe
P.O. Box PG 297, Paget 6,
Bermuda
Tel: 809-296-5274 or
Toll Free direct to hotel
800-468-1500

Hamiltonian Hotel and Island Club
P.O. Box HM 1738,
Hamilton 5, Bermuda
Tel: 809-295-5608

Harmony Hall Hotel
P.O. Box PG 299, Paget 6,
Bermuda
Tel: 809-296-3500

Mermaid Beach Club
P.O. Box WK 250,
Warwick 7, Bermuda
Tel: 809-296-5031

Newstead
P.O. Box PG 196, Paget 6,
Bermuda
Tel: 809-296-6060 or
Toll Free direct to hotel
800-468-4111

Palmetto Hotel and Cottages
P.O. Box FL 54,
Smiths Parish 3, Bermuda
Tel: 809-293-2323

Pompano Beach Club
32 Pompano Beach Road,
Southampton 8-01, Bermuda
Tel: 809-294-0222

The Reefs
56 South Road, Southampton
Parish 8-08, Bermuda
Tel: 809-298-0222

Rosedon
P.O. Box HM 290,
Hamilton 5, Bermuda
Tel: 809-295-1640

Stonington Beach Hotel
P.O. Box HN 523,
Hamilton 5, Bermuda
Tel: 809-296-5416

Waterloo House
P.O. Box HM 333,
Hamilton 5, Bermuda
Tel: 809-295-4480 or
Toll Free direct to hotel
800-468-4100

White Sands and Cottages
P.O. Box PG 174, Paget 6,
Bermuda
Tel: 809-296-2023

Cottage Colonies

Generally MAP is provided but other meal plans may sometimes be available upon request.

Ariel Sands Beach Club
P.O. Box HM 334,
Hamilton 5, Bermuda
Tel: 809-296-1010 or
Toll Free direct to hotel
800-468-6610

Cambridge Beaches
30 King's Point,
Sandys Parish 9-08, Bermuda
Tel: 809-294-0331 or
Toll Free direct to hotel
800-468-7300

Flamingo Beach Club
P.O. Box HM 466,
Hamilton 5, Bermuda
Tel: 809-296-3786

Horizons and Cottages
P.O. Box PG 198, Paget 6,
Bermuda
Tel: 809-296-0048 or
Toll Free direct to hotel
800-468-0022

Latana Colony Club
52 Railway Reserve,
Somerset Bridge,
Sandys Parish 9-20, Bermuda
Tel: 809-294-0141 or
Toll Free direct to hotel
800-468-3733

Pink Beach Club and Cottages
P.O. Box HM 1017,
Hamilton 5, Bermuda
Tel: 809-296-1666

The St. George's Club
P.O. Box GE 92,
St. George's 1, Bermuda
Tel: 809-297-1200

Willowbank
P.O. Box MA 296, Sandys 9,
Bermuda
Tel: 809-294-1616

Clubs (Private)

There are two private clubs in the resort category. Meal plans include BP and EP.

Coral Beach and Tennis Club
34 South Road,
Paget Parish 6-01, Bermuda
Tel: 809-296-2233

Mid Ocean Club
1 Mid Ocean Drive,
St. George's 1-22, Bermuda
Tel: 809-293-0330

Housekeeping Cottages and Apartments (Large)
This is the Bermudian way of saying 'efficiency units'. They are much like cottage colonies but without a main clubhouse. The majority are separate cottages, cottage units or wing of units, or apartment-type units with full kitchen for cooking all meals.

A few are situated in landscaped estates with their own private beach and pool. Others are designed in modern compact self-contained cottages or wings of units surrounding their own pool or overlooking their own beach or waterfront. Meal plan is EP. Travel agents can provide full particulars of several cottages and apartments.

Housekeeping Cottages and Apartments (Small)
These units usually offer fairly inexpensive accommodation in rather less spacious but comfortable surroundings. All have kitchen or kitchenette for full cooking facilities. A few have their own pool and terrace. Meal plan is generally EP (a few offer BP). Travel agents can provide full particulars.

Guest Houses (Large)
Most of the large guest houses are old Bermuda mansions modernised in the form of spacious bedrooms, dining area and lounge in the main house. One or two have bed/sitting rooms in separate or attached units in garden settings. An informal atmosphere prevails and there is no entertainment. Meal plan is BP (MAP sometimes available). The majority of the following fit into the above category although a few vary slightly in their facilities.

Guest Houses (Small)
Most bedrooms are located in the main house which is usually a private home. A few are located on the waterfront and have their own pool and patio. They offer comfortable and casual accommodation and there is no entertainment. Meal plan is BP (EP sometimes available).

Small Properties
Within this category are the smaller guest houses and house-

keeping cottages and apartments which usually are small private homes converted to accommodate fewer than twelve guests. Generally, the bedrooms are in the main house and/or adjacent structures with perhaps one or more housekeeping units. Many serve breakfast on request. Some are equipped with private kitchenette or have shared kitchen facilities for preparation of meals and snacks. Meal Plan is BP and EP.

Rentals
Finally there are various cottages, houses and apartments available for rental on a 'seasonal' or 'long term' basis to temporary visitors which are handled through Real Estate Agents in Bermuda. These private homes are completely furnished, but are not specifically designed as tourist accommodation. Many are located in select residential areas throughout the island. As they are usually private residences and not available on a regular basis, the locations vary each year, and beach and waterfront property cannot be guaranteed. 'Seasonal' rental is considered basically to be one week to three months. 'Long term' rental is normally six months or more.

TRANSPORTATION

Bermuda is small, excellent maps are readily available to tourists, and so an exploration plan can soon be made once the modes of travel have been considered. The major transport means are buses, ferries, motorbikes, and taxis though there are other interesting possibilities included in the following paragraphs.

Buses
An attractive and cheap way to see the islands is by the government-operated bus system. All routes serving Hamilton arrive and leave at the central bus terminal on Washington Street, just off Church Street a few steps east of City Hall. Bus rides from Hamilton to either side of the island cost around $2. Rides to the beaches on South Shore are also available and cost, depending on distance, $1 to $2. Bus passengers are

required to have the correct change in coins when boarding the bus. Children under three years of age ride free; under 13, for half price. Change, tokens, and bus schedules are available from the booth at the bus terminal. Bus tokens may also be purchased at any post office.

Ferries

Ferries provide a reliable and enjoyable way for visitors and Bermudians alike to commute daily from the Hamilton Terminal. Passengers may sail around Hamilton or take a longer trip to Somerset (about an hour round trip). Prices are economical – Hamilton to Somerset route is $2 each way, and features a snack bar on board. Hamilton-Paget-Warwick route is $1 each way. Bicycles are permitted on board. Route maps and schedules for buses and ferries are included in one freely available pamphlet titled 'Public Transport Bermuda'.

Motor-Assisted Cycles (Mopeds)

Mopeds are available for rent at cycle liveries throughout the island. Rental arrangements may be made through hotel and guest house management. The majority of cycle liveries are members of the Bermuda Chamber of Commerce and/or the Bermuda Cycle Association and they offer fairly uniform prices, quality, and service.

Visitors should remember the following: (a) read the rental agreement carefully before signing and familiarise yourself with the terms and conditions of the agreement; (b) by law third party insurance is compulsory but this only covers another party or cycle involved in an accident, not the rentor himself or his cycle; (c) rentors are liable for damage to their cycles or theft of the cycle or any parts, and cycle liveries may exercise their right to claim for damages or loss; (d) rentors are advised not to leave the cycle livery grounds until they are thoroughly familiar with how the cycle operates and the rules of the road. Most tourist accidents result from unfamiliarity with the machine and/or the roads; (e) it is illegal for children under 16 years of age to operate motor-assisted cycles and double-seated cycles are available to carry children or adults who prefer not to ride themselves; (f) the wearing of safety

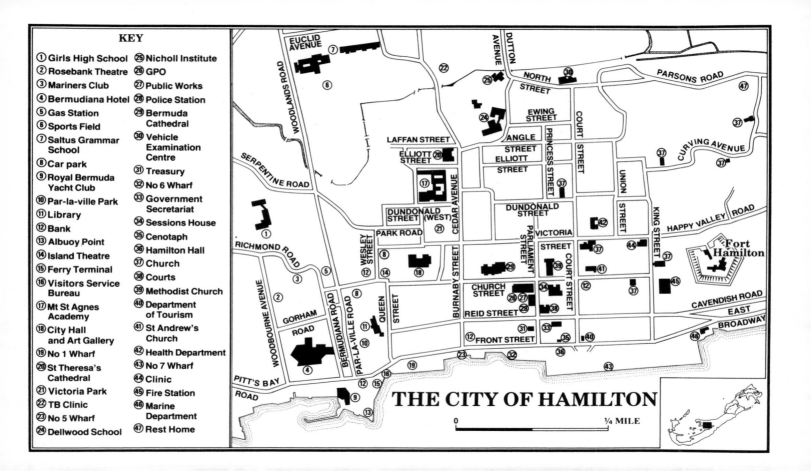

THE CITY OF HAMILTON

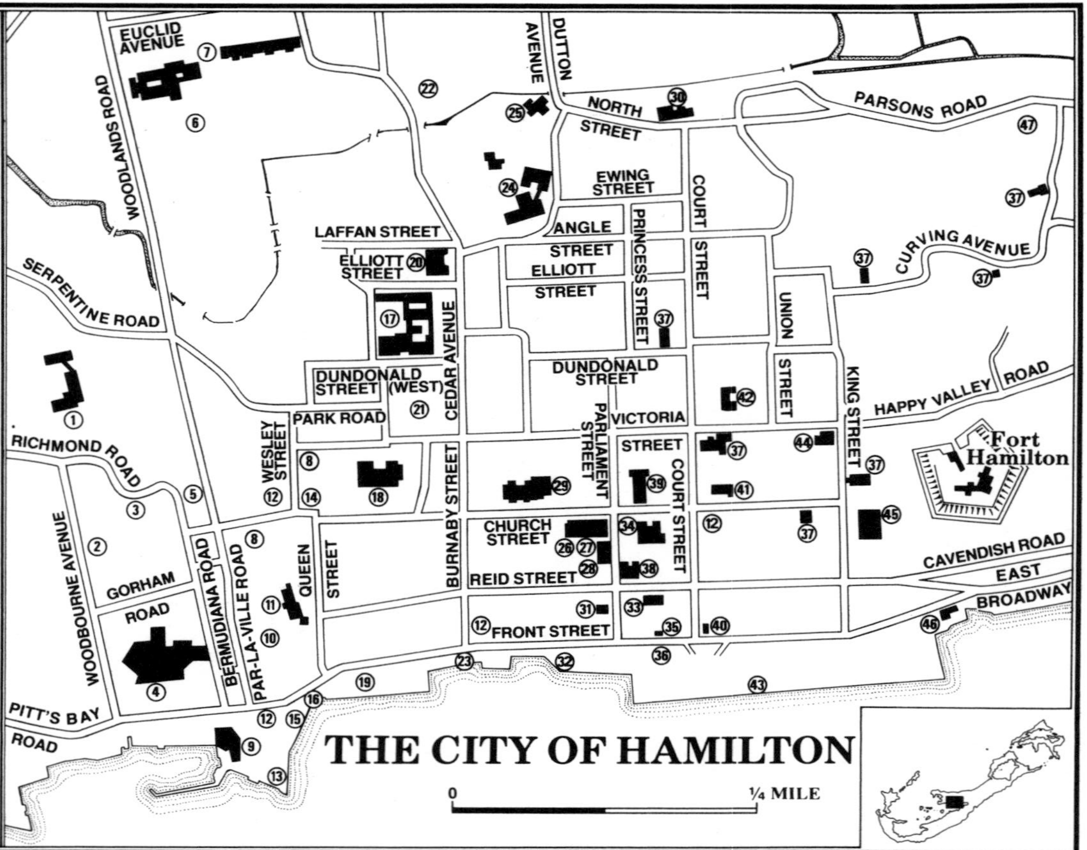

KEY

1. Girls High School
2. Rosebank Theatre
3. Mariners Club
4. Bermudiana Hotel
5. Gas Station
6. Sports Field
7. Saltus Grammar School
8. Car park
9. Royal Bermuda Yacht Club
10. Par-la-ville Park
11. Library
12. Bank
13. Albuoy Point
14. Island Theatre
15. Ferry Terminal
16. Visitors Service Bureau
17. Mt St Agnes Academy
18. City Hall and Art Gallery
19. No 1 Wharf
20. St Theresa's Cathedral
21. Victoria Park
22. TB Clinic
23. No 5 Wharf
24. Dellwood School
25. Nicholl Institute
26. GPO
27. Public Works
28. Police Station
29. Bermuda Cathedral
30. Vehicle Examination Centre
31. Treasury
32. No 6 Wharf
33. Government Secretariat
34. Sessions House
35. Cenotaph
36. Hamilton Hall
37. Church
38. Courts
39. Methodist Church
40. Department of Tourism
41. St Andrew's Church
42. Health Department
43. No 7 Wharf
44. Clinic
45. Fire Station
46. Marine Department
47. Rest Home

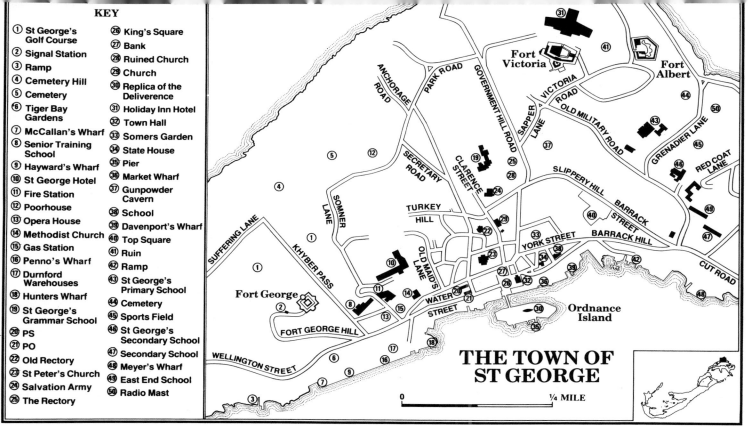

KEY

1. St George's Golf Course
2. Signal Station
3. Ramp
4. Cemetery Hill
5. Cemetery
6. Tiger Bay Gardens
7. McCallan's Wharf
8. Senior Training School
9. Hayward's Wharf
10. St George Hotel
11. Fire Station
12. Poorhouse
13. Opera House
14. Methodist Church
15. Gas Station
16. Penno's Wharf
17. Durnford Warehouses
18. Hunters Wharf
19. St George's Grammar School
20. PS
21. PO
22. Old Rectory
23. St Peter's Church
24. Salvation Army
25. The Rectory
26. King's Square
27. Bank
28. Ruined Church
29. Church
30. Replica of the Deliverence
31. Holiday Inn Hotel
32. Town Hall
33. Somers Garden
34. State House
35. Pier
36. Market Wharf
37. Gunpowder Cavern
38. School
39. Davenport's Wharf
40. Top Square
41. Ruin
42. Ramp
43. St George's Primary School
44. Cemetery
45. Sports Field
46. St George's Secondary School
47. Secondary School
48. Meyer's Wharf
49. East End School
50. Radio Mast

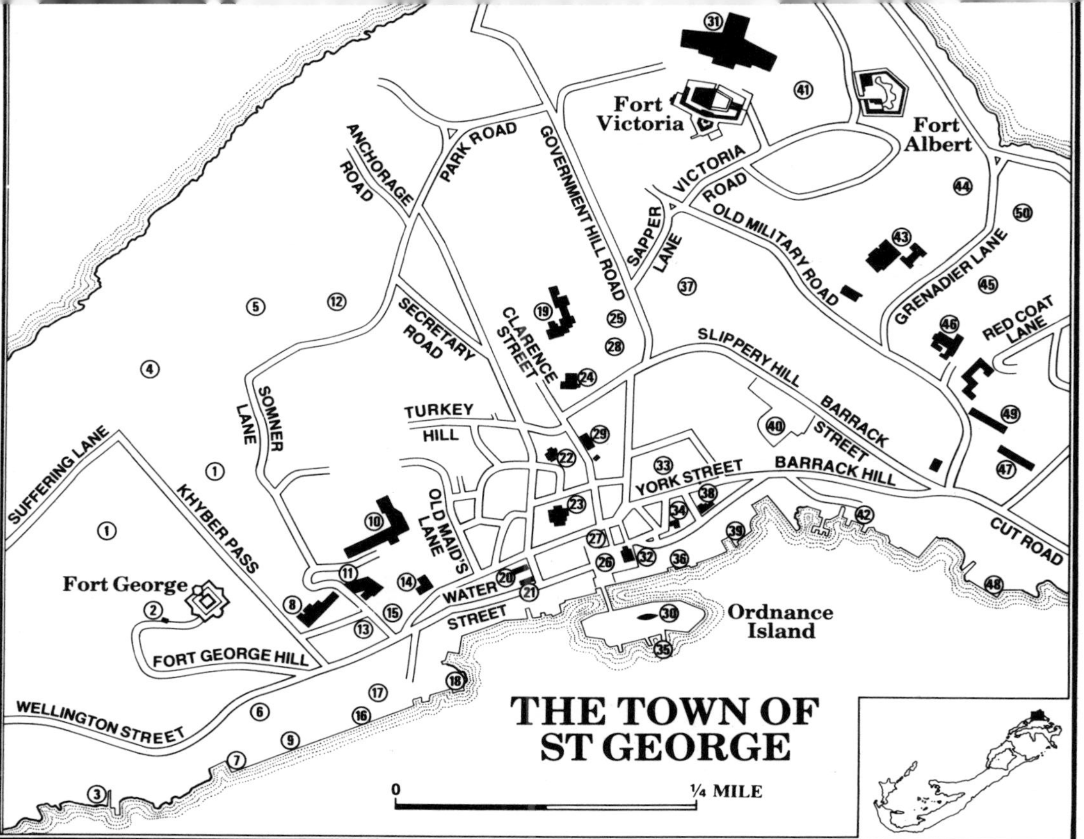

Bermuda: Street Maps of Hamilton and St. George's

helmets is compulsory by law for all cycle riders and cycle liveries must supply helmets to all riders (a refundable deposit is usually charged for helmets and locks/keys).

Taxis
Taxis are a most convenient mode of transportation. Each taxi is equipped with a meter, and is limited to four passengers. The first five-minute wait is free; then the meter is set at $1.20. Each additional minute is 18 cents. The fair is $2.40 for the first mile; $1.20 for each subsequent mile. Between midnight and 6 am there is a surcharge of 25 percent. Light luggage carried inside is free; there is a 25 cent charge for each article carried in the boot (trunk) or on the roof, with a maximum $3 charge. Bermuda's taxi drivers are helpful and friendly. Those displaying the Tour Guide flag are qualified tour guides for which the rate is $15 per hour with a three-hour minimum. Most taxi drivers are pleased with a 10–15 percent tip.

Airport Limousines
Airport limousines are operated by Bermuda Aviation Services. The 8-passenger mini-bus serves the smaller hotels and the 26-passenger coach serves the larger hotels, making several passenger stops en route. Pre-arranged bookings for the limousine service are requested. Fares are divided according to five zones.

Carriages
Motorization has reduced the number of carriages, but they are still very popular, and a part of the Bermuda atmosphere. They may be hired through hotel and guest house managers, or picked up on Front Street in Hamilton. Carriages are usually hired by the half hour.

Bicycles
Bicycles are an enjoyable and healthy way to see the island. Rental rates are reasonable – from about $5 a day to more favourable daily rates if week-long periods are booked.

Motorcoach Tours
Penboss Associates on Front Street offer special guided

motorcoach (tour bus) tours around the City of Hamilton and historic St. George's.

SIGHTSEEING

Bermuda's motto *Quo Fata Ferunt* – 'Whither the Fates Lead Us' – is one which leisurely visitors may well adopt as they slow down and travel from one end of the island to the other, enjoying the verdant marshes, the sparkling beaches, the homes nestled behind oleander shrubs, morning glory and hibiscus. The narrow, winding roads reveal surprises at every turn. Tourists should not be startled by the sound of tooting horns as they travel; it is not an expression of hostility, but rather an exchange of greetings between the islanders. Usually, vacationers do not have unlimited time to be led by fate so the following brief descriptions of places and things especially worth seeing provides a comprehensive summary from which choices can be made according to inclinations. The descriptions are presented in alphabetical order for ease of reference so that sightseeing routes and excursions can be planned.

Aquarium, Museum and Zoo

The Aquarium, opened in 1928, houses 26 tanks and one giant reef tank displaying over 75 species of fish and 50 species of marine vertebrates in a natural setting. The Museum contains exhibits covering Bermuda's geological development and growth and development of the island's eco-systems. The Zoological Gardens have a fine collection of tropical birds, monkeys, giant tortoises and alligators. A children's zoo – primarily small farm animals – is open in the summertime. Located in Flatts Village, 15 minutes from Hamilton.

(City Hall) Art Gallery

The Bermuda Society of Arts holds exhibitions throughout the year on the second floor of City Hall on Church Street in Hamilton. Many of the works of local and foreign artists are offered for sale.

Bermuda Arts Centre
Located directly opposite the Maritime Museum in the Dockyard at Ireland Island. There are choice exhibits and displays by a wide variety of local artists, some of which are for sale.

Bermuda Historical Society Museum
On the first floor of the Bermuda Library building on Queen Street in Hamilton. A small museum displaying antique silver, Bermuda cedar furniture, early Bermuda coins and costumes, and the sea chest and navigating lodestone of Sir George Somers.

Bermuda Library
On Queen Street in Hamilton. The reference department has virtually every book ever written about Bermuda. Collection of Bermuda's *The Royal Gazette* dates back to 1784. (A Junior Library is located on Church Street.)

Bermuda Cathedral
This Gothic-style cathedral on Church Street in Hamilton, was dedicated in 1894 and is the seat of the Church of England and the scene of the colony's state services. The imposing interior features impressive reredos, designed by the late sculptress Bylee Lang. It is constructed in granite, Italian marble, and Bermuda limestone.

Bermuda Pottery
Located at Blue Hole Hill in Hamilton Parish. Visitors are invited to watch lumps of clay grow into vases, figurines, and mugs in the hands of the potter. Clay sculptures are transformed into brilliant-coloured works of art after firing.

Blue Grotto Dolphins
At Blue Hole Hill, next to the causeway leading to the airport. Said to be one of the best shows of its kind in the world, the dolphins perform five shows a day in a natural setting. Tricks include surfing, diving for coins, basketball-playing, and acrobatics. Great family entertainment.

Botanical Gardens
Located off the South Shore Road in Paget, the gardens are planted with endemic flora as well as hundreds of well-marked shrubs and trees from around the world. The orchid and cacti collection is particularly outstanding. An unusual 'Garden for the Blind' features fragrant plants and herbs. On Tuesday, Wednesday and Friday (10:30 am), special tours are conducted from the restaurant parking lot.

Cabinet Building
This is a Hamilton landmark, occupying the block of Front Street between Court and Parliament Streets. It houses a number of government offices and is the site of the Convening of Parliament every autumn. Visitors are allowed into the Council Chamber where Bermuda's Upper House, the Senate, meets each Wednesday at 10 am (except during the summer recess). The handsome oak throne dates from 1642.

Carriage Museum
On Water Street in St. George's, a five-minute walk from King's Square. Until motorcars were admitted into Bermuda in 1946, carriages ruled the roads. On display are some of the 'ancestors' to those carriages.

Carter House
This historic house is one of the oldest stone buildings in Bermuda. It was built of limestone c. 1640 by the descendents of Christopher Carter, one of the first settlers from the shipwrecked *Sea Venture*. The cottage, located on St. David's, has been restored and is used as a museum of Bermuda culture and US military history. A pass can be obtained at the Number 1 Gate, US Naval Air Station in St. George's.

Confederate Museum
Located just off King's Square in St. George's. Formerly the Globe Hotel, it opened as a museum in 1961 and contains relics from the island's involvement in the US Civil War. The Globe Hotel was the headquarters of Major Norman Walker, the Confederate representative in Bermuda. There is a replica

of the Great Seal of the Confederacy fitted to a Victorian press so visitors can emboss their own as a souvenir.

Crystal Cave
Located on Wilkinson Avenue, near Blue Hole Hill in Hamilton Parish, visitors are guided to 90 feet below the surface through caverns of glistening stalagtites and stalagmites, and over a bridge floating on a crystal clear pool. Effectively lit, this natural setting is one of the most beautiful sightseeing attractions in Bermuda.

Devil's Hole
A former cave, this pool on Harrington Sound Road in Hamilton Parish, is fed by the sea through a quarter-mile of subterranean passages. Used as a natural aquarium since 1847, it is stocked with some 400 individual fish – including moray eels, sharks, giant groupers, and massive green turtles. Visitors tempt the pond's inhabitants with baited, but hookless, lines.

Deliverance (Replica)
Officially opened to the public in 1971, this is a replica of the first ship ever built in Bermuda – the original *Deliverance* was made from the wreckage of the *Sea Venture*. Exhibits on board include wax figures in the period's clothing and some objects the colonists brought with them from England. The *Deliverance* sits on Ordnance Island just off King's Square in St. George's.

Ducking Stool
Ordnance Island. This is a picturesque replica of the fiendish contraption used to punish wags and noisome wives.

Featherbed Alley Print Shop
The shop, on Featherbed Alley in St. George's, contains a working 18th century press on which the visitor can have a hand at printing a leaflet.

Fort Hamilton
On Happy Valley Road overlooking Hamilton and its harbour. During the middle of the 19th century, when Britain

and the US were not on friendly terms, several forts were constructed in Bermuda. Fort Hamilton was not completed until 1889, however, and was destined never to be used in war. In 1963, it was restored and opened to the public. The immense dry moat surrounding the fort is now a beautiful garden, and there is a tea shop serving lunches and teas. During Rendezvous Time – mid-November through March – the fort echoes the sound of bagpipes during the skirling ceremony which takes place each Monday.

Fort Scaur

This fort overlooks Ely's Harbour and the Great Sound in Somerset – a magnificent view. A 19th century fortress, it was built to protect the Royal Navy Dockyard on Ireland Island. Now a picnic ground, Fort Scaur is the site of a treasure hunt every Thursday during Rendezvous Time.

Fort St. Catherine

Located in St. George's, at the easternmost tip of the island. Wax figures in historic costumes lurk among the dark chambers; realistic historical dioramas and replicas of the British Crown Jewels can be viewed. The ramparts overlook the emerald waters of Sea Venture Flat where the first settlers were shipwrecked. This massive, thick-walled fort was part of an early defence system built in 1612 by Bermuda's first governor, Richard Moore.

Gibb's Hill Lighthouse

This imposing structure, on the South Shore in Southampton, was built in 1846 and is the oldest cast-iron lighthouse in the world. The magnificent view of the Bermuda islands and the sweeping shoreline from the look-out balcony at the top, is worth the 185-step climb. The workings of the impressive machinery is explained by the lighthouse keeper. Springtime visitors may be lucky enough to spot migrating whales beyond the south shore reefs.

Hamilton City Hall

Imposing white structure on Church Street in Hamilton. The

giant weather vane and wind cock tell maritime-minded Bermudians which way the wind is blowing. Completed in 1960, the building serves as headquarters for Hamilton's municipal government. The theatre on the first floor is the venue for theatrical, stage, music, and dance productions throughout the year. In addition, it is the site of Bermuda's annual Festival of the Performing Arts.

Leamington Caves

Located on Harrington Sound Road, Bailey's Bay, a five-minute ride from Crystal Cave. Extensive stalactite formations 65 feet below the earth's surface. Well-lit passageways and underground pools. Sightseers are given guided tours.

Maritime Museum

Housed in a 19th century stone building in Bermuda's old Royal Naval Dockyard (on Ireland Island), the museum carries memorabilia of the island's seafaring past. Opened by Queen Elizabeth II in 1975, the exhibits include displays of old Bermuda sailing craft, remnants and implements from Bermuda's old whaling industry, recovered treasure and artifacts removed from shipwrecks, the development of undersea diving, the history of piloting and commercial shipping. The Maritime Museum has also a restoration laboratory, boatbuilding workshop, extensive nautical library and countless maps, prints and paintings pertaining to the island's long nautical history.

Old Devonshire Church

This interesting church on Middle Road, halfway between Hamilton and Flatts Village, resembles an old Bermuda cottage from the outside. Inside, timbers and massive bolts are reminiscent of the early settlers' ship-building techniques. On the Sunday preceding Christmas, the church holds a colourful candlelight carol service.

Old State House

Believed to be the first stone structure in Bermuda, the Old

State House was built in 1619 of limestone and turtle-oil-and-lime mortar. It served for some time as the seat of the island's Parliament – the oldest in the British Commonwealth outside of the United Kingdom. Today, it is leased by a local Masonic Lodge for the token rent of one peppercorn per year, which is paid to the Governor in a colourful ceremony each April. Located on Princess Street in St. George's.

Palm Grove Gardens

These lavish gardens, located on the South Shore Road in Devonshire, were opened to the public in 1954 by the Gibbons family which still owns the estate. The section in front of the house, 'Palm Grove', is lush with vegetation, little ponds, and a moongate which serves as an entrance-way through the pretty trellised walk leading to a wishing well. The gardens are particularly beautiful in the spring and summer when they are amass with flowers. The public also has access to the small area behind the house where there is a small aviary and a bas-relief 'water-map' of the island.

Par-La-Ville Gardens

This charming little park is off Queen Street in Hamilton – in the heart of the shopping area, yet tucked out of sight. Once the private garden of William Perot, Bermuda's first post-master, it is a quiet spot for a boxed lunch beneath spreading palms and colourful golden shower trees.

The Bermuda Perfumery

Formerly the Perfume Factory, this is where Lili Perfumes are made. Visitors are given guided tours showing the perfume-making process, including the old method of extracting scents from native flowers. Among the fragrances produced: passion flower, Bermuda Easter Lily, oleander, jasmine and sweet pea. A mini Botanic Garden – open to the public, with a seating area and walkways – provides an attractive respite for visitors to this part of the island.

Perot Post Office

This handsomely restored building next to the Bermuda

Library on Queen Street in Hamilton, was once the home of Bermuda's first postmaster, William B. Perot. He improvised the island's first stamps and signed them; only 11 examples of these stamps are said to be in existence, some in Queen Elizabeth II's private collection.

St. George's Historical Society Museum
This building on Featherbed Alley in St. George's, dates from the early 1700's and contains an original 18th century Bermuda kitchen complete with utensils from that period. Exhibits include a 300-year old Bible, a letter from George Washington, and North American Indian axe heads. Some early settlers to St. David's Island were North American Indians, mainly Pequot.

St. George's Library
This is a circulation library set in an old 18th century Bermuda home, located in Stuart Hall on Aunt Peggy's Lane in St. George's. Cedar-beamed rooms and Bermuda-made furniture provide a cosy atmosphere.

St. Peter's Church
A small, interesting church on the Duke of York Street in St. George's is believed to be the oldest Anglican place of worship in the Western Hemisphere. Originally built entirely of cedar by the early colonists in 1612, it was almost destroyed by a hurricane in 1712. Some of the interior was, however salvaged and it was rebuilt in 1713. The original altar from 1624 is still in daily use. It has been restored many times and provides excellent examples of 17th, 18th, 19th and 20th century architectural work. Also in regular use is a silver communion service given to the church by King William III in 1697. There is a guide on duty except Sundays and holidays.

St. Theresa's Cathedral
St. Theresa's, on Cedar Avenue on the outskirts of Hamilton, is head of the Catholic churches in Bermuda. One of the island's prettiest churches, it was built in 1927 and is of Spanish design. It contains a silver and gold chalice presented

by Pope Paul VI to Bermuda's Roman Catholic diocese when he visited the colony in 1968.

Sessions House

Built in the 1820s, this Italian Renaissance-style structure with clock tower on Parliament Street in Hamilton houses the House of Assembly. Visitors may view the parliamentary debates from the public gallery every Friday morning, except during the summer recess.

Sir George Somers' Statue

This life-size statue of Bermuda's founder, sculpted by local artist Desmond Fountain, stands majestically on Ordnance Island, just off King's Square in St. George's. It was unveiled by HRH The Princess Margaret in October 1984.

Somerset Bridge

Believed to be the smallest drawbridge in the world (18in. span – just wide enough for the mast of a sailboat), Somerset Bridge connects the Bermuda mainland with Somerset Island, near the western end of the island.

Spittal Pond and Spanish Rock

Spittal Pond, some 60 acres of woodlands and meadows, can be seen from the South Shore Road in Smith's Parish. A National Trust property, it is the island's largest wildlife sanctuary. A 'must' on the sightseeing trail for picnic lunches and exploration of the scenic walkways along the high shoreline cliffs and rocks and through the lush wooded areas. November–April is the best time to view migrating birds. Spittal Pond also shelters Spanish Rock, which bears inscriptions made by a mariner in 1543. Some historians, however, feel he may have been Portuguese, not Spanish.

Springfield Library

'Springfield,' on Middle Road in Somerset, is a 17th century Bermuda home comprising of a group of small buildings. Restored by the National Trust, it houses the Somerset Library and is bordered by the Gilbert Nature Reserve, which provides a perfect place for a leisurely and peaceful stroll.

Stocks and Pillory
On King's Square, St. George's. Another old punishment device for the miscreant, recalls a by-gone era. It's fun to photograph!

Town Hall, St. George's
The original structure of the King's Square building was erected in 1782 and has been restored twice since, with extensive use of native cedar. It is the home of the Corporation of St. George's.

Tucker House
This charming, restored 18th century cottage on Water Street in St. George's was the original home of the prominent Tucker family. It is filled with fine antique furniture and silver, family portraits and heirlooms. During the US Civil War, the present kitchen served as a residence of the town barber, Joseph H. Rainey, a former American slave who, after the war, became the first black member of the US House of Representatives. A special room has been provided for Mr. Rainey's memorabilia.

Verdmont
Located on Collector's Hill off the South Shore Road, five minutes' ride from Flatts Village. The mansion was built in the mid-17th century by an early governor of Bermuda, Capt. William Sayle, and restored by the National Trust in the 1950s. It is furnished throughout with an outstanding collection of antiques. The cedar staircase is considered the finest in Bermuda.

Visitors' Service Bureau
On Front Street (next to the Ferry Terminal) provides free information, brochures, maps, and any additional advice.

Waterville
On Harbour Road, just outside Hamilton, 'Waterville' is the headquarters of the Bermuda National Trust. An early 18th century Bermuda home, its gardens contain a collection of local and exotic trees.

SPORTS AND PHYSICAL RECREATION

When the outdoor sportsperson on vacation discovers Bermuda he or she soon realises that the island offers year-round action in the wide range of sports described in Chapter 3. Everything is available from scuba diving to sailing to world famous deep-sea fishing. Plus tennis, cycling, jogging, horseback riding, and more golf per square mile than any island on earth. Particulars are listed in the 'Bermuda Sportsman's Guide' which is issued by the Department of Tourism and is freely available to visitors.

On Beaches

Of course, many recreational activities can be carried out free of charge on Bermuda's glorious beaches. The islands provide some of the world's most beautiful and unusual beaches for walking, swimming, snorkelling, jogging, ball games, and horseback riding. The turquoise waters lapping the pink beaches, with the azure sky as a backdrop, make the most idyllic vacation setting. It is difficult to choose between beaches of such extraordinary beauty but, generally speaking, the best beaches are on the South Shore from Southampton to Tucker's Town. Some are long sweeps of unbroken sand; others are divided by low coral cliffs into protected little coves. Only a few hotels and guest houses are located directly on the ocean, but since the island is only 2.41 km (1.5 miles) at its widest point, beaches are easily reached by bicycle or taxi. Guests not staying at beach properties can either dress for swimming at their hotel, wear their sports clothes on top of their bathing suits and bicycle to any one of the small or large beaches which are open to all visitors; or they may go to a beach club to change. Their hotel or guest house management will advise them about convenient beaches and how to get there. It is important to note that there are no life guards on the public beaches at any time, however, most private beach clubs have beach attendants certain hours of the day.

During the months 1 November–15 March the beach facilities (listed below) may not be as extensive and the hours of operation of the beach clubs/houses may be reduced somewhat. Some beach clubs/houses may close completely for several weeks during this time.

ELBOW BEACH HOTEL, Paget
Open daily. For non-house guests there is a small charge which includes a locker and towel, use of the changing rooms, and fresh-water showers. Informal lunches and snacks served at Surf Club. Lunch 12:15–3:00 pm; snacks only 3:00–4:00 pm. Two bars, one in club (open 11:00 am–6:00 pm) and one on beach (open 12 noon–3:00 pm).

HORSESHOE BAY BEACH HOUSE, Southampton
Open daily: 9:00 am–5:30 pm weekdays, and 9:00 am–6:30 pm weekends. Full snack bar. Use of beach, patio and rest rooms free.

SHELLY BAY BEACH HOUSE, Hamilton Parish
Open daily, all year, 10:00 am–7:00 pm. Full snack bar. Changing rooms available at no charge.

SOUTH SHORE BEACH CLUB, Warwick
Open daily until 5:00 pm. There is a small charge for non-house guests which includes locker and towel. Complete luncheon facilities. Bar open 11:00 am–5:00 pm during March–June, and 11:00 am–6:30 pm during July–October.

SHOPPING

Fine selections of china, pottery, crystal, woolens, linen, and imported clothing are available in Bermuda and often at favourable prices. Although the main concentration of shops is in the City of Hamilton, leisurely shopping can also be enjoyed in the old town of St. George's, in Somerset, and in some major hotels. And then there are the small shops scattered around the parishes. Everywhere visitors receive the advantages resulting from low tariffs on imported luxury goods, with no sales tax of any sort. Bermuda currency is always quoted, and credit cards are honoured at most shops. Quality merchandise, the keystone of island shopping, has long been traditional, and it continues today.

Americans should note that gifts under $50 may be sent

home without limit, to friends and relatives in bona fide properly labelled gift packages, as long as no more than one package is sent to any one individual on the same day. These do not count in $400 duty-free quotas. Canadians visiting Bermuda may send back home gifts up to the value of $20 without the recipient having to pay duty. Bermuda shop assistants are conversant with the regulations, and wrapping and mailing are usually available.

There are worthwhile savings in Bermuda on all merchandise imported from Great Britain and Europe. However, visitors are advised to check prices at home of any merchandise in which they are particularly interested, so as to provide a basis for comparison with prices in Bermuda. Bermuda prices cannot compare with some discounted prices of goods in North America. Visitors should also compare quality of items; quality in Bermuda is usually high. Bermuda is not a duty-free port.

Though not an exhaustive list, the following gives some ideas on what to look for in the shops.

Antiques

Some interesting buys, mostly English. Note the export of Bermuda-made antique items is restricted by law.

Bermuda-Made Goods

Not extensive but unusual items in Bermuda cedar wood, paintings, and other art forms in a variety of media, silk-screened materials, jewellery, etc.

Cameras

Good savings on cameras over standard US retail prices but may not be competitive over US discount prices.

China

Excellent savings on many English and European china items.

Clothing

Worthwhile savings on cashmere sweaters, camel's hair sweaters, Harris tweed and Jaegar coats, doeskin slacks and skirts, Daks slacks and other clothing from Great Britain.

Crystal
Excellent savings on many crystal items.

Golf Balls
Excellent savings.

Leather Goods
Excellent savings on best quality British leather goods in the higher price bracket.

Linens
Excellent savings on linen from Ireland, Madeira, etc.

Liquor
In Bond – good savings. Minimum purchase 2-litre packages. Liquor will not be served in Bermuda to anyone under 18 years of age.

Perfume
French perfumes cheaper than in US.

Silver
Savings on English sterling, plate, and antique silver. Worthwhile savings on Danish flatware.

Watches
Worthwhile savings on Swiss watches and clocks.

Woollens
Finest British woollens at good savings.

Yardgoods
Excellent selection of Irish linen, Liberty silks, and cottons, Madras cottons, silks, etc.

NIGHTLIFE

There is a good variety of evening and night-time entertainment in Bermuda each night of the week throughout most of the year. There are several English-style pubs with entertainment, and a few night-clubs and discos; most of the resort hotels have their own night-clubs, some also have a disco, and they all have cocktail lounges, bars and patios for a variety of parties and light entertainment; and, most of the smaller hotels and cottage colonies also have cocktail lounges, bars and patios for parties and light entertainment.

Entertainment abounds during the summer season but between December and the end of March the availability of entertainment everywhere is minimal. Some hotels, pubs, night-clubs and discos close completely; the ones which do remain open through the winter months may curtail their entertainment or may provide entertainment only certain nights of the week, and will reduce cover charges or will not impose a cover charge at all during this time.

Cover charges are usual in all night-clubs, discos and occasionally in some of the pubs – for the latter it depends on what group is entertaining. Reservations are advisable in advance for the night-clubs both in and out of hotels. In most cases the night-clubs and discos both in and out of the hotels require gentlemen to wear jackets, and in some cases a tie as well. For the pubs' and the hotels' other evening/night-time activities such as barbecues, swizzle parties, etc., the atmosphere is more relaxed and casual to smart-casual dress is suitable and acceptable. However, it is always wise for visitors to check in advance on dress requirements with the establishment concerned.

Dancing, Floor Shows and Other Activities

There is dancing nightly in all the resort hotels from approximately 9:30 pm until 1:00 am or later in the hotels' bars or cocktail lounges, outside terraces or patios, and also in their night-clubs before and after show time. The hotels' night-clubs are open most nights of the week and feature a different local show each show night, some offering two shows. The show times are approximately 10:30 pm and 1:00 am and feature either a limbo show, fire dancers, steel band, calypso band or a musical variety band. Some hotels offer international performers – their first show features local artists and the second show features an international performer or group.

Other activities provided for the house guests throughout the week beginning in the early evening include swizzle parties, travelogues, barbecues, Bermuda films and feature-length movies, cinema horse racing, and Bermuda arts and crafts exhibitions.

In the smaller hotels and cottage colonies many interesting and talented smaller groups and entertainment personalities appear most nights of the week. The entertainment is very often held outside on a terrace or patio during the summer months and cover charges are not usually imposed. Other activities provided for the house guests throughout the week beginning in the early evening include swizzle parties, travelogues, barbecues, buffets, films, etc.

There are several English-style pubs which are open seven days a week from approximately 11:00 am until 1:00 am for lunch and dinner. Most nights of the week entertainment is offered by a pianist or guitarist or sometimes a duo beginning at approximately 9:00 pm until 1:00 am and patrons can enjoy the entertainment while dining or just sitting at the bar. Usually folk and country singers entertain as well as English-style sing-a-longs.

SPECIAL EVENTS

Finally, throughout the year, Bermuda plays host to a wide variety of events and activities. For those who may like to visit the islands at a particular time, a brief outline of the 1986 special events is recorded here.

Rendezvous Time

Every year, between 15 November and 31 March, Bermuda welcomes visitors in a very special way. There is a daily series of events ranging from the ceremonial noonday gun ceremony in St. George's each Wednesday to a treasure hunt through the western parishes each Thursday. At Fort Hamilton pipers, drummers, and dancers perform the Skirling Ceremony; local artisans exhibit their wares in a Market Day and cycle rides and fun runs provide a 'rendezvous' between visitors and Bermudians. Of course, all the natural and other attractions are available as well – apart from those previously noted as being closed at this time. Special events during Rendezvous Time are the Pro-Am Goodwill Golf Tournament, Christmas and New Years festivities, the International Square Dance Convention, the International Marathon and Ten Kilometre Race, a Regional Bridge Tournament, the Rendezvous Bowling Tournament, Super Senior Tennis Tournament, Bermuda Dog Shows International and more.

College Weeks

Bermuda College Weeks is the name given to the annual spring fling for thouands of collegians from North America. Dates change each year and are based on college vacation dates. Activity during the College Weeks centres on a free weekly programme arranged and paid for by the Bermuda Department of Tourism. The activities begin on Sunday night and run through Friday. Beach parties, free lunches, and boat cruises are among the activities included in the programme. Entertainment includes calypso, rock bands, limbo show, and a steel band concert. Admission to these events is by complimentary 'College Week Courtesy Card' issued to all bona fide college students. These are given to students, upon presentation of their student identification cards.

There are no youth hostels, YWCAs or YMCAs in Bermuda, and camping and sleeping on the beaches is not permitted at any time. Though some hotels do not accept student groups, a majority of the visiting collegians are accommodated in the properties that are licensed by the Bermuda Government. Students are very aware of budgets and Bermuda, during College Weeks, offers special rates at hotels and guest houses, restaurants, pubs and nightclubs exclusively for students. An accommodation rate sheet is available from the Department of Tourism.

College Weeks are not destructive or disturbing to other Bermuda visitors. Generally the visiting students represent only 20 percent of all visitors on the island and the parties move each day. Bermuda College Weeks is over fifty years old with traditions such as the College Week Queen Contest, mopeds, boat cruises, and the Bermuda Strollers. Students learn very quickly that 'Bermuda is Another World.'

The Bermuda Department of Tourism issues promotional College Week literature and posters and has available for loan a 15-minute College Week film on 16 mm or video tape.

Bermuda Festival
January/February – a 6-week International Arts Festival featuring world-renowned theatrical performers specialising in classical music, dance, jazz, drama, and entertainment.

Bermuda International Marathon and Ten Kilometre Race
January – with international and Bermudian runners.

Regional Bridge Tournament
January/February – sponsored by Bermuda Unit of the American Contract Bridge League.

Bermuda Dog Shows International
March – held in a week of competitions featuring dogs from Bermuda and other countries.

Open Houses and Gardens
April/May – beautiful Bermuda homes and gardens open to visitors every Wednesday afternoon.

Beat Retreat Ceremony
The Bermuda Regiment and Massed Pipes, Drums and Dancers. Held on Front Street, Hamilton at 9:00 pm on last Wednesday each month of April through October except August; and in King's Square, St. George's at 9:00 pm the first Tuesday of each month of April through October except August.

Invitational International Race Week
April/May – yachtsmen from US, UK, and Canada compete with Bermudians in races in six to seven classes of boats.

Peppercorn Ceremony
April – His Excellency the Governor in historic and traditional ceremony collects the annual rent of one peppercorn for use of the island's old State House in St. George's.

Agricultural Show
April – A 3-day exhibit of Bermuda's best fruits, flowers, vegetables and livestock and featuring equestrian and other ring events.

Bermuda Game Fishing Tournament
1 January–31 December – now held year round – with awards presented for top catches in 26 varieties of game fish. All amateur anglers eligible. No entry fee and no fishing licence required.

Bermuda Heritage Month
May – a month of cultural and sporting activities to commemorate Bermuda's heritage, culminating on Bermuda Day, 23 May, 1986 a public holiday when Bermudians traditionally head for the beaches for the first time of the year.

Queen's Birthday Parade
14 June, 1986 – public holiday held on June 16 with military parade on Front Street, Hamilton.

Newport Bermuda Yacht Race
June (even years) – Newport R.I. to Bermuda. About 180 of the world's finest yachts compete in this famous blue-water classic.

Bermuda Ocean Race
June (even years) – 45 blue-water racing and cruising yachts compete from Annapolis, MD to Bermuda.

Operation Sail '86
June – part of the celebration of the 100th Anniversary of the Statue of Liberty. Tall ships and ocean-going yachts from Europe gather in Bermuda the week of 16 June, and depart 22–24 June for New York Harbour.

Bacardi Rum Match Yacht Racing Championship
26–28 June, 1986. Last world-class match racing before the '87 America's Cup.

Cup Match and Somers Day
31 July, and 2 August, 1986 – public holidays – a spectacular 2-day cricket match between east and west ends of the island.

Bermuda Hockey Festival
10–14 September, 1986 – International field hockey tournament.

Etchell–22 World Match Yacht Racing Championship
October – top international skippers from USA, Europe and Bermuda compete in a round-robin series.

International One Design Class Invitational
October – held in Bermuda.

Convening of Parliament
November – His Excellency the Governor opens Parliament with traditional ceremony and military guard of honour.

Bermuda Dog Shows International
November – held in a week of competitions featuring dogs from Bermuda and other countries.

Remembrance Day
11 November – the day is marked with a parade of Bermudians, British and US military units, Bermuda Police and Veterans organisations, in honour of the men who died in service of their country.

Invitation Tennis Week
November – more than 100 visiting tennis players compete with Bermudians in two weeks of singles and doubles matches.

Bermuda Goodwill Tournament
December – a week of golfing activity as 90–100 pro-amateur foursomes from international golf clubs compete in this best-ball tournament played over 72 holes on four of Bermuda's eight courses.

7 PROSPECTS

Having traced and described Bermuda's physical characteristics, history, modern life, social environment, economy, and its paradise-isle features, a brief analysis of future prospects will be attempted. The discussion centres on the people of Bermuda for it is their views and actions which will ultimately determine Bermuda's fate.

QUALITY OF LIFE

In the autumn of 1982 a group of social scientists tentatively concluded that Bermuda had substantial social problems. However, in presenting their findings to the Government they conceded that their conclusions were matters of opinion about which there was little firm information and they recommended that a systematic inquiry should be conducted. Thus, in May and June of 1984, the Government commissioned a survey designed to determine Bermudians' own perceptions of their 'Quality of Life' and their related concerns about public issues. It was probably the first quality of life survey ever commissioned by a national government which was intended to guide public policy. Professor T. R. Gurr, Payson S. Wild Professor of Political Science at Northwestern University, conducted the inquiry and some of his major findings and conclusions are presented here.

A representative sample of island residents aged 15 and over was interviewed by telephone between 28 May and 14 June 1984. Virtually all Bermudian households have telephones and the great majority of residents proved willing to answer questions. Such conditions help to make telephone interviewing a reliable technique for surveying people's attitudes. The survey results were weighted using demographic variables to bring the sample into correspondence with the published figures in the 1980 Bermuda Census. This is a standard technical procedure used to ensure that the tabulated answers reflect all social groups in proportion to their numbers in the population.

The questionnaire used was designed in consultation among Bermudian officials and social researchers at Northwestern University in Evanston, Illinois. The interviewing was done by trained Bermudians and the data were analysed by Gurr so that the report now offers a portrait of the current personal and social concerns of a representative cross-section of island residents. It also indicates what people think about the Government's priorities and policies. What emerges is a more diverse and a more positive picture than the consultants saw. Perhaps most important, there is little basis for pessimism – most Bermudians have a positive outlook on their lives and their country, and a clear sense of the kinds of issues that require public attention.

Of those surveyed, only 16 percent were unemployed (and most of them were still at school or retired men and women of both races). Generally, Bermudians have a high degree of satisfaction with the quality of life in Bermuda. Overall, more than three-quarters (77 percent) are very or somewhat satisfied, 17 percent somewhat dissatisfied, and only 5 percent are very dissatisfied. White Bermudians are somewhat more likely to be satisfied than black Bermudians – 90 percent compared to 69 percent. The dissatisfied 22 percent of Bermudians are more likely to be women than men and to be in the 21–40 age bracket. This may reflect the particular discontents of women who are single parents.

While it is generally true that blacks are somewhat less likely to be satisfied than whites, black youths in the 15–21 age bracket are more satisfied than their elders and closer to their white peers in satisfaction than in any other age group. Family income evidently has little to do with overall satisfaction. In families with reported incomes less than $15,000, the 'satisfied' outweigh the 'dissatisfied' by 74 percent to 25 percent, while for families over $25,000 the difference is 83 percent to

17 percent. This suggests that for poorer Bermudians, psychic satisfactions may compensate for less-than-average incomes. Another way to make this comparison is to analyse the income brackets of the 'dissatisfied' minority. A third of them are in the upper-income bracket and another third in the $15–$25,000 bracket, evidence for the familiar truth that money does not necessarily bring happiness.

Most Bermudians, whatever their personal satisfactions, think that life in Bermuda is better than elsewhere. 72 percent think it is better than in the United States, Canada, and Britain; 17 percent think it is the same and only 7 percent think Bermuda is worse. Compared with Caribbean islands, nearly 80 percent think Bermuda is better and most of the rest do not know. There is very little difference between blacks and whites or men and women in these general perceptions. Even among the 'dissatisfied' 22 percent of Bermudians, the great majority think that the quality of life in Bermuda is as good or better than elsewhere.

But there is a tiny minority of Bermudians who are both dissatisfied with their quality of life and think life in Bermuda is worse than in North America or Britain. They are only 6 percent of the total population.

People were also asked about their sense of progress during the last five years and their expectations about changes in the next five years. People rated their past, present, and hoped-for future standard of living. The majority, black and white, rate past, present, and future as 'good' or 'excellent.' And there is a sense of progress: 'excellent' ratings increase from past to present to future, while 'fair' ratings decline. Blacks are somewhat less positive than whites in their ratings for each point in time, but they share a sense of personal progress.

People's perception of improvement or decline in their standard of living also was measured by comparing their ratings of past, present, and future. The results are strongly positive: three-quarters or more see their standard of living remaining the same or improving. Only 16 percent rated their present standard of living worse than five years ago, while 23 percent thought their personal future would be worse than the present. About a quarter of poorer Bermudians – those in the lowest family-income bracket – think that their standard of living is worse. But few of them expect it to get worse in the future. In fact they are somewhat more optimistic than people in higher-income households about their future standard of living. When differences in family income are taken into account, black and white Bermudians are very similar in these perceptions of change in their standards of living.

People also were asked to compare their personal quality of life with those of other Bermudians, and to assess their personal freedom and independence. Virtually no Bermudians, even the most dissatisfied, think that their quality of life is worse than that of other Bermudians. This suggests that very few Bermudians feel a sense of deprivation when comparing their lives with others'. More than half think their situation is the same as others', while about a third in every category think they are better off. No significant differences among groups were evident in the answers to this question.

There were detectable differences among groups, however, in freedom and independence. On the positive side, nearly three-quarters of people (77 percent of whites, 70 percent of blacks) answered excellent or good. On the other hand, 30 to 35 percent of adults aged 21–40 are people with low incomes who thought their freedom and independence were only fair or poor. This may be a consequence of material concerns or lack of personal economic opportunity: it is to be expected that people struggling to keep up with the rising cost of living will feel more constrained than others. The answers to these questions also provide some insights into the concerns of the 22 percent who are generally dissatisfied with their quality of life.

Other evidence shows that most of the attitudes and concerns of the discontented generally resemble those of satisfied Bermudians. No one common cause for their discontent can be identified. In short, they do not seem to share a sense of relative deprivation. Rather, their discontent probably arises mainly from individual situations, for example among single parents struggling to hold a job and raise a child, or ambitious younger men in jobs with few prospects for promotion. In Bermuda, however, discontent is not associated in any consistent way with poverty or material deprivation, or with racial discrimination.

The best things about living in Bermuda are psychic satisfactions: the friendliness of its people and its natural beauty. These qualities were said to be most important by 31 percent and 23 percent respectively of all respondents, while another 10 percent mentioned a third psychic satisfaction, personal freedom. Material aspects of life were mentioned less often: 17 percent cited the economy, 9 percent mentioned low taxes, and 6 percent said security was most important. Bermudians of both races, all age groups, and all income levels were in close agreement on the relative importance of these qualities.

The worst things about living in Bermuda vary with race and age. White Bermudians and young people of both races are most concerned about the islands' small size. As is to be expected, people in the lower income groups are most concerned about the high cost of living. Overall, 27 percent said cost of living was the worst aspect, 18 percent cited small size, and 14 percent said housing. The other specific problems mentioned by 3 percent or more of people were drugs (6 percent), unemployment (3 percent), racial tension (3 percent), and traffic (3 percent).

Issues of middling concern to Bermudians are labour relations (23 percent think they are being handled poorly), the outlook for the elderly (22 percent), and protection of the environment (18 percent). People are most satisfied with health care, police service, the management of the economy, and their present housing conditions.

A brief look at the concerns of the dissatisfied 22 percent of Bermudians shows that they consistently give worse ratings to the handling of every social issue. What is striking is that they agree almost exactly with the satisfied majority in the rankings of their concerns. For example, they give the poorest ratings to control of drug abuse and recreational facilities, and the best ratings to health care – the same rankings as 'all Bermudians'. This indicates that the 'syndrome of discontent' is not caused by one or a few particular social problems, with the possible exception of housing. The causal connection is probably the other way round – personal discontent makes people less satisfied with the handling of all social issues.

The Bermudian educational system, public and private, gets high marks from parents of school children. The survey identifies only a few issues for concern, particularly a desire for more homework and more school discipline. The majority of parents are well-satisfied with their child's school. Discipline is not thought to be much of a problem, although a quarter of black parents and a quarter of parents of private-school children think discipline is too lenient. Almost all whites give a positive rating to the quality of teaching in their child's school. Black parents are somewhat more concerned: one quarter of them say that teaching is only fair. But not a single parent surveyed said discipline was too strict, or the quality of teaching poor.

Given the high level of satisfaction with the schools, it is not surprising that no major problem area emerged when people were asked what aspect of the educational system most needed improvement. The most common answer, for all groups, was teaching, but it was mentioned by only a fifth of parents. White parents are more concerned about discipline, especially in the private schools. A fifth of black parents want examinations improved, one in ten wants better facilities. These two areas are of little concern to white parents.

RACE RELATIONS

Continuing with Gurr's findings it is seen that Bermudians differ somewhat along racial lines in their satisfactions and dissatisfactions, and also in some of their perceptions about social and economic issues. Very few of them (5 percent of whites, 2 percent of blacks), however, thought that racial tension was Bermuda's worst problem.

The researchers asked many direct questions about race relations, prejudice, and discrimination. These are the two most positive conclusions. One is that most Bermudians agree that there has been substantial recent progress in race relations. The other is that white and black youths are closer together in nondiscriminatory attitudes and experience, and think that racial discrimination is less a problem, than older Bermudians. But the results also show that, for all social groups, prejudice and discrimination remain a matter of concern.

The first issue is whether Bermudians all think about prejudice and discrimination in black–white terms. When asked about discrimination the pattern of answers among the Portuguese and English are virtually the same as those among whites generally. And people of Caribbean origin respond similarly to blacks generally. The inference is that race is more important than national heritage in shaping Bermudians' perceptions of race relations. Caribbeans or Portuguese may have some distinctive ethnic attitudes and experiences, but evidently think about prejudice and discrimination in racial terms.

Nearly two-thirds of Bermudians say that they socialize equally with members of both races, 31 percent mainly with members of their own race. Blacks and whites report similar experiences, which helps confirm the accuracy of this portrait of high levels of interracial interaction. The highest levels of interracial socializing are reported by white and black youths. The lowest levels are found among higher-income white men.

The Extent of Prejudice

Just under half of Bermudians think that most whites are prejudiced against blacks, and that most blacks are prejudiced against whites. What one group believes about another group is not necessarily true, however. Whereas most blacks (53 percent vs 39 percent) think that most whites are prejudiced, most whites (60 percent vs 34 percent) think that other whites are not prejudiced. Whites also are rather hopeful about black attitudes toward them: 51 percent say blacks are not prejudiced against whites compared with 41 percent who think blacks are prejudiced against them. Among blacks, however, the picture is reversed: 49 percent of blacks think other blacks are prejudiced against whites, slightly more than the 44 percent who think blacks are not so prejudiced.

The general pattern, in short, is that blacks perceive somewhat more racial prejudice, among themselves and among whites, while whites optimistically see somewhat less prejudice in themselves and blacks. Education certainly has a key role to play here.

The Future

The groups who consistently perceive the greatest amount of prejudice in blacks and in whites are older blacks and black women. The groups who consistently see the least prejudice are youths, both black and white. These differences offer hope for the future. Older Bermudians carry the burdens of the past, young people have had the experience of growing up in a more open multi-racial society.

The picture of Bermudians' hopes and fears for race relations in future generations indicates that three-quarters of all people think that relations between black and white children are better than those between adults, while most others think it is the same (16 percent). The great majority (71 percent) also think there is more prejudice among adults than among young people. And there are no significant differences among groups in these positive views. The one real basis for concern is that half of Bermudians still think it is easier for a white child to get ahead in Bermudian society, while only 41 percent think that there is no racial difference. Black youths and younger black adults are the most pessimistic about equal opportunities.

Discrimination

Prejudice, real or perceived, does not necessarily translate into discrimination. But most Bermudians think that racial discrimination is a problem; they disagree mainly in how serious. One person in six (16 percent) thinks discrimination is a very serious problem – blacks more than whites. A plurality of 44 percent think discrimination a somewhat serious problem, with no significant differences among groups. Another 38 percent thinks discrimination is not particularly serious – whites more than blacks. Here again is evidence of generational change: young Bermudians, black and white, tend to think that discrimination is a less serious problem than older people.

Another positive indication is the widespread sense that race relations have improved during the last five years, a point agreed upon by nearly half of every group in the population. Only one in 10 residents thinks they have become worse. Those who said they thought race relations had improved were asked how satisfied they were with the rate of progress. Only 13 percent were dissatisfied with the rate of progress; the great majority of those who think there has been progress, 84 percent, are very or somewhat satisfied on this count.

People also were asked whether they thought there was discrimination in each of eight specific areas of employment and services. Half or more of all blacks and a quarter or more of all whites say they think there is some discrimination in each area. The problem is thought to be greatest in hiring and promotion by private businesses and hotels. Government is thought to be fairer in hiring and promotions. The most positive ratings are given to fairness in the schools and government services.

These results are not convincing because the survey did not ask what specifics were in the minds of the 40 percent to 60 percent of respondents who thought there was 'some' discrimination in every area mentioned. Perceptions of discrimination, although a cause for concern, are not the same as the practice of discrimination. Some whites may think there is discrimination by blacks against whites, rather than vice versa. And it is possible that many Bermudians say there is discrimination because other people say it exists. Who discriminates against whom, in what specific ways, needs to be asked in future surveys. It is possible that many Bermudians' perceptions of discrimination are a legacy of the past rather than a reflection of their own contemporary experience.

The 60 percent who said they thought discrimination was a very or somewhat serious problem were asked whether government could do anything about it. There was little support for a more active government role. Half of both whites and blacks said 'nothing'. The other responses show that the most common prescription is 'individual change', recommended by 19 percent, which implies little or no government involvement. A more active public role is supported by those who recommend legal action (10 percent), Bermudianisation and integration (5 percent each), and 'government involvement' generally (11 percent). Of the 60 percent who are concerned about discrimination, 33 percent mention one of these kinds of government action. These 33 percent make up only 20 percent of all people surveyed. There is little difference among races in these performances. And youths are the least likely to recommend further government action.

These results should not be interpreted as opposition to any government role in race relations. Rather, most Bermudians evidently do not want government to add to its responsibilities in this area. Bermuda probably has followed a similar pattern to the United States, where substantial public support developed during the 1960s for government action against discrimination. Once new civil rights policies were in force, however, support for further government intervention declined.

GOVERNMENT AND POLITICAL PARTICIPATION

Most Bermudians accept the way in which the Government spends tax money. Nearly a third (31 percent) think it is good or excellent. 38 percent say it is fair, while 25 percent rate it poor or very poor. Since Bermuda has no income tax, the 'fair' and 'poor' ratings probably reflect the prevailing fashion in most Western societies to be sceptical of what government does. For some people, though, they may reflect a deeper cynicism about government. Scepticism about government is part of the contemporary political worldview of people in most Western countries. In the United States between 1958 and 1978, those trusting in government decreased from 58 percent to 19 percent of the population while cynics increased from 11 percent to 52 percent. Cynicism is present but seems somewhat less in Bermuda, perhaps because the population is small enough that ordinary citizens are more likely to know and interact with officials and politicians. Two major qualifications about these results also need to be repeated. First, they may be influenced by partisan attitudes toward the present Government, both pro and con.

Second, and more important, majorities of Bermudians agree that they can affect what happens in government. This is one of the virtues of politics in a small, democratic country: most people think that their participation can make a difference.

Not in the report, but perhaps an important issue, is the belief held by some that economic power exists independently of political power. Thus, some argue, that though élite whites may have conceded political power they, nevertheless, hold on to economic power. The same sceptics, with others, also favour independence for Bermuda while the remainder counter 'independence from what?' The majority seem well satisfied with the present situation and the majority view is likely to hold fast in this tiny democracy. At this point it is useful to remember that democracy is a dreadful way to govern but it is the best there is!

PROSPECTS FOR CIVIL DISORDER

In earlier parts of this book it has been made clear that civil disorder can be disastrous for Bermuda's economy, and it can threaten the viability of the country. This is a prime issue when considering Bermuda's prospects. So what does Gurr's study conclude in this regard?

Summarising and concluding, the survey gives ample evidence that substantial majorities of Bermudians are satisfied with life on the islands and are optimistic about the future. People are generally satisfied with the quality of life on Bermuda. 70 percent think that their standard of living is good or excellent, 77 percent think it will be the same or better five years from now. 71 percent think that conditions in Bermuda are the same or better than they were five years ago, 73 percent think they will be the same or better in five years. 86 percent of employed people are satisfied with their jobs. 85 percent think that race relations are the same or better than they were five years ago. This widespread satisfaction with life in Bermuda is balanced by concern about a number of social issues, some cynicism about government and politics, and the existence of a minority who are dissatisfied. This is the information which makes possible a concluding assessment of the prospects for civil disorder.

Much has been made of the causes of civil disorder in Bermuda's recent history. Some argue that the roots of future violence are to be found in relative deprivation arising from inequalities in wealth and status. Others have pointed to widespread cynicism about government and to underlying tensions in race relations. The survey does not have evidence to address all these arguments, but, as Gurr points out, his results do strongly suggest that there is at present no large or explosive potential for disorder because:

(1) Most Bermudians are satisfied with their lives, their work, and prospects for the future. The minority of Bermudians who have what has been labelled a 'syndrome of discontent' have no one or two common sources of deprivation. Most of their discontents appear to arise from individual circumstances. In particular, there is no evidence that their discontent arises mainly from racial differences or material deprivation.

(2) Dissatisfied Bermudians are distinctly more cynical about government and politics than satisfied Bermudians. But they are no more likely than other people surveyed to approve of forms of political action like demonstrations and boycotts. Nor are they significantly more likely to approve of political violence. In fact, 90 percent of the dissatisfied minority do not approve of violent political action.

(3) There is a high degree of support among all Bermudians, discontented or not, for such forms of political action as demonstrations and boycotts. Sizeable minorities have participated in them in the past. But this support for political action is no more closely related to political cynicism than it is to dissatisfaction.

(4) The conventional account of the causes of political disorder in multiracial societies begins with inequalities and poverty, especially along racial lines. These then translate into a shared sense of relative deprivation and feelings of intense discontent. The survey shows that while some Bermudians are discontented, these are not its main sources.

(5) The next step in the explanation links discontent with

attitudes of antagonism toward government and beliefs that disruptive political action is justified. The survey shows that among Bermudians, such links are incomplete or non-existent. While discontented Bermudians are relatively cynical about government, very few approve of violent action.

(6) An alternative link in the explantion of disorder attributes it directly to political cynicism and hostility toward government, whether or not fueled by discontent. This link also is missing in Bermuda: politically-cynical Bermudians are just as unlikely as other Bermudians to endorse violent action.

(7) There is potential for protest in Bermuda in the form of demonstrations and boycotts, just as there is in almost every other Western society. Given the state of the Bermudian psyche in 1984, that potential will be realized, if at all, in situations of political and economic contention. It is unlikely to be a reaction to deep-rooted grievances because such grievances as exist are mostly individual rather than collective. And unless protest organizers misjudge, or authorities over-react, protests are unlikely to lead to riotous violence. The great majority of Bermudians, satisfied or not, disapprove such action and think it counter-productive.

THE LAST WORD

Having studied Bermuda, experienced its life, and compared it with many regions of the world, this writer firmly believes that the island is another 'Jewel in the Crown' but without any major, or insurmountable, flaws. Gurr concluded that 'Bermudians need to be convinced that the future can be as good or better [in Bermuda than anywhere else].' If Bermudians can take their National Trust's advice and fit tourism into Bermuda (rather than the other way round), emphasise the quality of the Bermuda vacation, fully differentiate service to visitors from servitude to visitors, and solicit visitors' aid in preserving the islands' environment and cultural integrity, then Bermuda can become what former Governor Sir Peter Ramsbottom forecast, '. . . a model for the world in terms of race relations as well as economics.'

BIBLIOGRAPHY

Bell, E. Y. *Beautiful Bermuda*, 5th ed, New York and Bermuda, Bermuda Tourist and Advertising Bureau, 1913

Benians, E. A., Butler, J. and Carrington, C. E. (Gen Eds) *The Cambridge History of the British Empire* (Vol III), Cambridge, University Press, 1960

Bermuda. *Bermuda Report 1980–1984*, Hamilton, Department of Public Relations, 1986

Bermuda Historical Quarterly

Bermuda Official Gazette

Butland, G. J. *Bermuda: A New Study*, New York: Vantage Press, 1980

Colonial Office (C.O.)

C.O. 37. Original Corr. 1689–1939. 289 vols

C.O. 334. (Ind. 12925–30, 15383–4, 17725, 18838–9, 19147–8.) Register of Corresp. 1850–1926, 13 vols

C.O. 38. Entry Books of Out Letters, 1615–1872, 38 vols

C.O. 449. Register of Out Letters, 1872–1926, 6 vols

C.O. 39. Acts, 1690–1936, 43 vols

C.O. 40. Sessional Papers, 1687–1940, 116 vols

C.O. 647. Gov Gazettes, 1902–40, 9 vols

C.O. 41. Miscellanea, 1715–1940, 140 vols

Field Officer, *Bermuda: A Colony, A Fortress, and a Prison: or, Eighteen Months in the Somers' Islands*, London, Longman, Brown, Green, Longmans, & Roberts, 1857

Gurr, T. R. *The Quality of Life and Prospects for Change in Bermuda: A report to the Government of Bermuda on a Sample Survey*, Hamilton, The Cabinet Office, 1984

Hannau, H. W. *The Bermuda Isles*, London: Robert Hale, 1978

Hayward, S. J., Gomez, V. H., Sterrer, W. (Eds) *Bermuda's Delicate Balance: People & the Environment*, Hamilton, The Bermuda National Trust, 1981

Heyl, J. B. *Bermuda Through The Camera of James B. Heyl 1868–1897*, Hamilton: The Bermuda Book Stores, 1951

Hughes, L. *A Letter From The Summer Islands*, London, 1615 (Printed in London by I. B. for William Welby), New York, Don Capo Press, 1971; Amsterdam, Theatrvm Orbis Terrarvm, 1971

Ives, V. A. (Ed) *The Rich Papers: Letters From Bermuda 1615–1646*, Toronto, University of Toronto Press, 1984 (For Bermuda National Trust.)

Jickells, S. 'Plants and Animals' in Hayward *et al.*, *op. cit.*, pp. 154–166

Jourdan, S. *Plaine Description of the Barmvdas*, London, 1613 (Printed by W. Stansby, for W. Welby). Amsterdam, Theatrum Orbis Terrarum, 1971; New York, Da Capo Press, 1971

Kennedy, J. *Biography of a Colonial Town: Hamilton, Bermuda 1790–1897*, Hamilton, The Bermuda Book Stores, 1961

Kennedy, J. *Isle of Devils: Bermuda Under the Somers Island Company 1609–1685*, London, Collins, 1971

Kerr, W. B. *Bermuda and the American Revolution: 1760–1783*, Princeton, Princeton University Press, 1936 (Reprinted by Anchor Books, 1969)

Kusche, L. D. *Bermuda Triangle Mystery – Solved*, London, New English Library, 1981

Manning, F. E. *Black Clubs in Bermuda: Ethnography of a Play World*, Ithaca & London, Cornell University Press, 1973

McCallan, E. A. *Life on Old St. David's, Bermuda*, Hamilton, Historical Monuments Trust, 1948

Mercer, J. E. *Bermuda Settlers of the 17th Century*, Baltimore, Genealogical Publishing, 1982

Morley, C. *Notes on Bermuda*, New York, Henry, Longwell and Another, 1931.

Palmer, Margaret (Ed. R. V. Tooley) *The Mapping of Bermuda: A Bibliography of Printed Maps and Charts 1548–1970*, 3d rev. ed., London, Holland Press Cartographica, 1983

Paul, M. *Black Families in Modern Bermuda*, Göttingen, Fed. Rep. of Germany: Edition Herodot, 1983

Robinson, K. E. *Heritage*, London: Macmillan Education, 1979

Rose, J. H., Newton, A. P., Benians, E. A. (Gen Eds) *The Cambridge History of the British Empire* (Vols I & II), Cambridge, University Press, 1960

Smith, J. E. *Slavery in Bermuda*, New York, Vantage, 1976

Sterrer, W. (Ed) *Marine Fauna and Flora of Bermuda*, New York, John Wiley, 1986

The Times (London), 12–16 Mar, 1973; 1–7 Dec, 1977

Tucker, T. *Bermuda: Today and Yesterday 1503–1980s*, London, Robert Hale, 1983; Bermuda, Baxter's, 1983

Weatherill, J. *Faces of Bermuda*, Warminster, Wilts, Morrell Wylye Head, 1985
Wilkinson, H. C. *The Adventurers of Bermuda: A History of the Island from its Discovery Until the Dissolution of the Somers Island Company in 1684*, London, Oxford University Press, 1933 (2nd ed 1958)
Wilkinson, H. C. *Bermuda in the Old Empire*, London, Oxford University Press, 1950
Wilkinson, H. C. *Bermuda From Sail to Steam*, Vol 1 (1784–1818), London, Oxford University Press, 1973
Wilkinson, H. C. *Bermuda From Sail to Steam*, Vol II (1819–1901), London, Oxford University Press, 1973
Wingate, D. B. 'Conservation Laws' in Hayward *et al. op.cit.*, pp. 295–306
Wyers, S. 'Fresh Water' in Hayward *et al. op.cit.*, pp. 123–136
Zuill, W. *Bermuda Sampler, 1815–1850*, Hamilton: The Bermuda Book Stores, 1937
Zuill, W. S. *The Story of Bermuda and Her People*, 2nd Ed, London, Macmillan, 1983

ACKNOWLEDGEMENTS

I am particularly grateful to The Hon. John W. D. Swan, Premier of Bermuda, for supporting this book project from the outset. He kindly elicited the support of all Government departments to give me any information I wanted, and he arranged for me to use the data contained in many government publications (including Professor Gurr's report). Of prime benefit was the *Bermuda Report 1980–84*, edited by Valerie E. Smith, who also gave me supplementary advice in an interview. Other Bermudian politicians and civil servants I wish to thank for their help are: The Hon. Robert V. Barritt, Minister of Community and Cultural Affairs; The Hon. T. Haskins Davis, Minister of the Environment; The Hon. Sidney R. Stallard, Minister of Transport; David Critchley, Permanent Secretary, Ministry of Health and Social Services; R. A. Hunt, Administrator, Ministry of Transport; I. W. Hughes, Permanent Secretary, Ministry of the Environment; Edward A. Manuel, Director, Department of Agriculture and Fisheries; Lowdru H.

Robinson, Director, Department of Community Services; Charles H. Webbe, Department of Tourism; and, the Economic Advisor of the Ministry of Finance.

The Premier supported my desire to be objective in discussions I had with him and demonstrated his willingness to be non-political in this venture by assigning Brian Darby, Director, Department of Information Services, to assist me as an inquiring journalist might. Mr. Darby went beyond the call of duty in his assistance and I am most grateful to him.

Too many Bermudians for me to name them all kindly answered my questions in an open and friendly manner. Some, however, helped in ways which call for more than general acknowledgement and are: Colin Anderson; Teddy Brangman; Elizabeth M. Ward, The St. George's Club; Jay Wold, General Manager, The Princess Hotel; J. V. Zuill, The Bermuda Book Store; and, W. S. Zuill of The National Trust.

Much of the work on this book was carried out, among other tasks, when I was a Senior Research Scholar in Social and Administrative Studies at Corpus Christi College, Cambridge during the Summer of 1986. The generous hospitality of The Master and Fellows was greatly appreciated by me as also was the kindness and friendship of Christine McCrum. Additionally, the Cambridge University Library was the source of many of the books and documents I consulted. Similarly, I continue to appreciate all the support I receive from many sources in the University of Victoria, British Columbia. Particularly the excellent secretarial services given to me for the past five years by Mrs. Sharon Kucey.

INDEX

INDEX